D0643341

The Chambers
of
the Palace

The Chambers
of
the Palace

Teachings of Rabbi Nachman of Bratslav

Y. David Shulman

JASON ARONSON INC.
Northvale, New Jersey
London

The author gratefully acknowledges permission to reprint the following:

Asamer B'Sh'vochin, from REBBE NACHMAN'S SONGS, Vol. I:1, *The Traditional Music of Chasidei Breslov, Shabbos Evening: Part I*, pp. 38–39. Copyright © 1988 by Breslov Research Institute. Reprinted by permission of Benzion Solomon and the Breslov Research Institute.

This book was set in 11 pt. Caslon by Lind Graphics of Upper Saddle River, New Jersey, and printed by Haddon Craftsmen in Scranton, Pennsylvania.

Library of Congress Cataloging-in-Publication Data

Nahman, of Bratslav, 1772–1811.
    The chambers of the palace : teachings of Rabbi Nahman of Bratslav
/ by Y. David Shulman.
        p. cm.
    Includes bibliographical references and index.
    ISBN 0-87668-180-1
    1. Hasidism. I. Shulman, Yaacov Dovid. II. Title.
BM198.N25 1993
296.8'332 – dc20   92-35707

Manufactured in the United States of America. Jason Aronson Inc. offers books and cassettes. For information and catalog write to Jason Aronson Inc., 230 Livingston Street, Northvale, New Jersey 07647.

Contents

Foreword
by Dr. Hillel Seidman

This book satisfies a timely need. In an age of noisy shallowness and dumb superficiality even in dealing with the sublime heights and unfathomed profundity of Torah, Y. David Shulman has managed to penetrate the roots of Bratslav and to grasp its outwardly expanding branches. He has rediscovered the relevant relations between reality and religion.

Through the prism of these pages, the reader pierces cosmic mysteries. Yet what one peers at is merely the overflow of the innermost Torah lights, glimpses of flashing sparks of the flames that burn inside.

Shulman has undertaken a daring task. It takes a good deal of audacity and effort to gain entrance to the inner quality of Rabbi Nachman's lofty teachings and tales and to bring out in monumental simplicity his profound thought, making it reachable to everyone.

Rabbi Nachman is a poet and philosopher overpowered by overwhelming faith and Torah imperatives. The anthologizer has placed in a common orbit Rabbi Nachman's rational analysis, mundane earthiness, and all-encompassing synthesis of ideas.

The land of Israel is elevated in Bratslav thought to the heights of sanctity and incandescent spirituality. Yet Rabbi Nachman never lost sight of the earthly Jewish homeland, saying, "The land of Israel is these fields and houses. . . ."

This book mirrors the individuality of this unique *tzaddik* and his solitary conduct. Not only the people of Israel "dwell alone" but also this *tzaddik*. But he is never truly alone, for his meditations are permeated by the all-encompassing Divine Presence.

Thus has the anthologizer molded into a harmonious unity Rabbi Nachman's diverse and often contradictory teachings: complexity and simplicity, burning passion and cold rationality, fiery feeling and detached thought, heart and mind.

This book *proves* that the author achieves its lofty task.

Acknowledgments

This book is dedicated to all the people in my life who have helped guide me to the path where no highwayman lies in wait and helped me feel the yearning of the heart of the world. (Of course, responsibility for the contents of this book rests solely with me.)

There are too many for me to name, but I would like to at least acknowledge in writing a few and beg indulgence of those whom I have not mentioned: Arthur Kurzweil; Simchah and Ruth Frischling; Daniel and Chana Goodman; Yankel and Pessi Dinnerstein; Dr. and Mrs. Hillel Seidman; Rabbi Chaim Friedman; Rabbi Myer Fund; Rabbi Moshe Sokol; Rabbi Michael and Chashie Skobac; Shimon and Cindy Lanzbom; Ruchama King; Yochanan and Gillian Gordon; Steven Blumberg; Rabbi Yechezkel and Rachel-Leah Grunwald; Chaim Radin; Gad and Nama Frenkel; Rabbi Aharon and Mindy Parry; Dr. Shelly Halpern; Amnon Nissan; Aharon and Shoshanah Shamberg; Dr. Gershon and Tovah Rubin; my parents, Avraham and Chana Shulman, and my sister, Chava; the students at The Flame (New York University); Rabbi Shlomo Freifeld of blessed memory; Leibel Rochman of blessed memory; Gordon Victor of blessed memory; Rabbi

Dovid Din of blessed memory; all those who weave evocation and open the door of perception; and finally, Rabbi Nachman, who still is dancing in the woods of the soul at midnight:

You walked into the apple orchard to be born,
Below the golden mountain, your hands were all torn,
And singing of joy, you looked so forlorn,
And you went dancing in the woods at midnight.

Playing chess with your jacket laid down on the ground,
You raised up your eyes and you looked all around;
There's a kind of a cry that doesn't make any sound
When you're dancing in the woods at midnight.

In the middle of the night, the world disappears,
No one hears a sound but the man without ears.
The king who's surrounded by jokers and jeers
Goes dancing in the woods at midnight.

A foot becomes an angel that becomes a hand,
You look on a map for the promised land,
Sifting tears for a message in the sand
That goes dancing in the woods at midnight.

There is no despair, you cried, don't forget,
You threw back your head and cried out with regret.
The sound of that cry is echoing yet
And goes dancing in the woods at midnight.

If you believe you can break, then believe you can fix,
Believe you can rise from the stones and the kicks,
Believe you can see through the sleight-of-hand tricks
And go dancing in the woods at midnight.

There's nothing as whole as a broken moan,
Water will wear away the toughest stone,
You said, I will never leave you alone,
And you went dancing in the woods at midnight.

You said, It's not over, the coal will keep burning,
The words will keep flying, the world will keep turning,
So keep your hands clean and keep your heart yearning
To go dancing in the woods at midnight.

Introduction

Rabbi Nachman of Bratslav (1772–1810), great-grandson of the founder of Chasidism, the Baal Shem Tov (1700–1760), was himself a pivotal figure in the evolutionary process of Jewish spirituality. The Baal Shem Tov taught a heart-felt path of Torah based on an inclusive love of all Jews. His teachings stressed the ability of all Jews to serve God in joy, and the new customs of Chasidism provided a means for Jews to feel a camaraderie with each other and a connection to *tzaddikim*, spiritual masters.

Two generations later, Rabbi Shneur Zalman of Liadi (1745–1812), founder of Lubavitch (or Chabad) Chasidism, systematized the teachings of the Baal Shem Tov and organized a solidly and broadly based chasidic community. The Baal Shem Tov's original sparks were now developed into a long-burning fire that could serve many Jews for many generations. Chasidism was institutionalized. The original flame of enthusiasm was now filtered through intellectual and ordered understanding and developed as a complex philosophy.

At the same time, Rabbi Nachman was developing the teachings of his great-grandfather in a different direction. Rabbi Nachman was a poet, an individualist, a man who operated through his heart, a man filled with passion, a man filled with the youthful fire of breaking through all structures in order to get to God, not a man who wished to consolidate structures.

Rabbi Nachman did not attempt to organize the Baal Shem Tov's teachings; rather, he attempted to take them to the next level. He was a man of passions and simple striving to serve God; he was a man of poetry and imagination, a man of holiness and holy longing, a man of feeling, a man of titanic inner struggles, a man of impulse, brutal honesty, deep love, a man who was forever struggling, growing, joyous, suffering, human, and holy. Rabbi Nachman's teachings reached out, awakened the flame within a person's heart to race toward God. And then Rabbi Nachman's techniques of serving God gave a person the tools with which to channel that fiery enthusiasm: for instance, the stress on joy, on broad and all-inclusive learning without intellectual self-doubt, and, perhaps most of all, the championing of *hitbodedut*, lone, spontaneous prayer to God, ideally in a forest in the depth of the night.

Rabbi Nachman was a man who, seized with the passion of his pure vision of true service of God, could not compromise with the establishment; he could not allow the concern for whose feelings he might ruffle, whose toes he might step on, to interfere with his work. More than that, Rabbi Nachman was not averse to stating the great worth of his path and his own greatness. Although this may seem egotistical, and therefore nonholy, this was actually in a tradition of spiritual masters, as recorded in the Talmud and elsewhere, who have spoken frankly of their greatness.

Thus, although Rabbi Nachman was accorded great respect by many of the leading *tzaddikim* of his day (such as the above-mentioned Rabbi Shneur Zalman, Rabbi Levi Yitzchak of Berditchev, and others), his uncompromising exterior gained him adversaries. Rabbi Nachman soon became the center of great dispute.

Although the town with whose name Rabbi Nachman's teachings are identified is officially known as Bratslav, the followers of Rabbi Nachman prefer the spelling of Breslov because, as Rabbi Nachman pointed out, in Hebrew the letters can be rearranged to spell "a heart of flesh" (Ezekiel 26:26) (see Chapter 17). I would have wished to employ the spelling favored by Rabbi Nachman; however, publishers prefer the other spelling, which is considered more "scientific."

Rabbi Nachman transmitted his teachings not only in conventional ways, but also related tales, dreams, visions, and parables.

The following allegory can be interpreted in various ways to gain insight into Rabbi Nachman's path of serving God, one that he called "a new path that is really very old":

A man once left his father and spent a very long time among others in foreign lands. Finally, he returned home and boasted that he had attained great skill in making chandeliers. He said that he would like all the chandelier-makers to gather together so that he could show off his expertise.

When the man's father brought together all the chandelier-makers, he displayed one of his chandeliers. But they all thought that it was very ugly.

When his father asked them to give him their frank opinion, they were forced to admit that the chandelier was displeasing.

But when the man heard this, he replied, "That's exactly my point. What one person considers ugly, another person approves of. And what that second person approves of is disliked by the next person. Whatever one person finds ugly another thinks is beautiful, and vice versa. I made this chandelier out of flaws in order to show everyone that one isn't perfect, and that every individual is flawed. Whatever one finds beautiful another thinks is incomplete.

"But the truth of the matter is that I can make a chandelier correctly."

If they were to know all the flaws and missing parts of the thing, they would know its quality. But they never really saw it.

Great are God's acts. Nobody is identical with anyone else. All human forms were included within man, *Adam* – within the very word "Adam." The same holds true for everything else: all lights were included in the word "light," and so forth. Even every tree leaf is unique.

Rabbi Nachman spoke about this at great length.

He said that there are such wisdoms in this world that one could live on them and not require food or drink.[1]

I. One can interpret this parable as follows:

The man refers to God as He acts in this world. The other craftsmen are *tzaddikim* – holy men. God has created the world, and within it He created man with flaws. The flaws that one sees in others mirror one's own internal incompleteness. Only the son, the *tzaddik* who looks at a human being and recognizes that the flaws that he sees mirror his own internal imperfections, is truly a *tzaddik*. One must love others with a nonjudgmental, empathetic compassion.

Rabbi Nachman's teachings stress finding the good in oneself and others. The primary characteristic of the leader – the *tzaddik* – is his compassion.

Rabbi Nachman's teachings offer a path for those who have felt themselves to be on the lowest rungs.

II. From a different angle, one can stress the fact that in this parable, the chandelier-maker, the *tzaddik*, is an artisan.

Rabbi Nachman's teachings have a particular appeal to the artistic, creative individual. Rabbi Nachman was himself a poetic and idiosyncratic personality whose Bohemian spirit expressed itself in a number of ways. From his childhood, he loved to roam in the forests and fields alone, communing with God, and he later institutionalized this as the system of spontaneous prayer called *hitbodedut*. He reported dreams and visions and told brilliant allegorical tales that are supreme examples of the imagination deeply integrated with mystical consciousness.

His teachings are often poetic and playfully associative. His startling leaps of intuition, connecting apparently unrelated topics, are expressions of nonlinear, right-brain thinking. Rabbi Nachman makes great use of clever word play and ideational association. (In English translation, this technique becomes laborious, and so teachings with such elements are here under-

---

1. *Sippurei Maasiyot* (Brooklyn: Hasidei Breslov, 5736), appendix.

represented.) Rabbi Nachman's brilliance is like a Mozartian tour de force.

Related to this, Rabbi Nachman identified himself with King David (of whom he was a descendant). King David's psalms are individual expressions of self, and so King David is the Jewish model of the creative personality.

The championing of individual expression implies a clash with the model of a homogenous, group identity. Some Torah leaders express an Orthodox, national voice. Their task is to offer a clear, broad path for their followers. But a minority of leaders, such as Rabbi Nachman, are individuals in a state of tension with the group mentality.

As such, Rabbi Nachman teaches an offbeat Torah that constantly challenges his followers in fundamental ways.

Actually, Rabbi Nachman was both individual and orthodox; his broad personality encompassed both the individual and communal aspects of Jewish living.

Unfortunately, however, those who admire and study him often limit his scope. Rabbi Nachman's Orthodox admirers generally tend to be noncognizant of Rabbi Nachman's genius as an artistically creative personality. And those secular intellectuals and artists who are drawn to his originality and brilliance are not aware of how his teachings fit into the structure of the Torah.

It is relatively easy to be a creative, even spiritual, personality without having to fit into a framework greater than oneself – e.g., a Torah way of life. It is equally easy to lead a Torah way of life that has no relationship to artistic creativity. In either case, such a person can only partially appreciate Rabbi Nachman's teachings. Rabbi Nachman's teachings gain their three-dimensional power because they encompass a tension between these two modes of being.

III. One may also interpret this parable as follows:

The chandelier-maker is the true *tzaddik*.

The *tzaddik* is not understood by the other leaders, or lesser *tzaddikim*, who have not traveled spiritually or conceptually as he has. They too are experts who are involved in making chandeliers that spread light. Yet it has been God's will that this *tzaddik* alone gain achievements distant from those of the others.

The other leaders do not understand him, and they project their failings as well as their strengths onto him. They do not realize that it is his role to serve as a lightning rod and catalyst for them.

Therefore, each leader, although seeing some good in the *tzaddik*, declares him to be deficient overall.

But the *tzaddik* declares that he is also capable of making a perfect chandelier typical of the *tzaddik*.

The *tzaddik* appears this way not only in the eyes of other leaders, but in the eyes of people who are involved in a life of spiritual growth, in a life that tries to bring light into the world.

Some people are both attracted to and disturbed by Rabbi Nachman. One person finds Rabbi Nachman's stress on *hitbodedut*—isolated, spontaneous prayer—inspiring, but is disturbed by Rabbi Nachman's statements regarding physicality. Another finds Rabbi Nachman's radically spiritual view a refreshing relief from materialism but is disturbed by Rabbi Nachman's self-praise. A third person finds that this self-praise strengthens his appreciation of Rabbi Nachman's authority and shows him what to strive for in his own life, but he finds Rabbi Nachman's championing of *hitbodedut* to be interfering with his struggle to communicate better with others.

Rabbi Nachman is an enigma. He presents himself as the exemplar of the great *tzaddik*. Yet at the same time he tells his followers that he cannot serve as a model for them to emulate. He declares that anyone can reach the level of spirituality that he reached, but declares his uniqueness as well.

Rabbi Nachman tests those who come to his path by acting as a figure against which they may project their weaknesses.

Rabbi Nachman appears as one of the first teachers of popular psychology. His teachings stress self-esteem, simple striving, self-application. Yet they are simultaneously not simple at all. They make statements, they contain constructs that seem to have no analogue in everyday life, nor even in the standard constructs of Torah theory.

Rabbi Nachman's teachings are a combination of the simple

and the opaque, of Torah for the *tzaddik* and Torah for the most simple person.

His teachings may appear to be marvelously simple and inspiring. But the simplicity is unsatisfactory, a mask for something deeper. Rabbi Nachman said that neither his adversaries nor his followers understood who he is. Rabbi Nachman remains mysterious forever. He is accessible and inaccessible.

At one moment, Rabbi Nachman is comforting; at another, maddeningly problematic. He is there, and yet he is not there. He gives an answer, and when one comes to him he suddenly vanishes into a wisp.

He drew his followers close to his heart and sacrificed himself for them. Then he told them that they have no connection to him and he could cast them off as simply as blowing feathers off his coat.

He says something that one seems to understand, yet when one examines it, it seems to have shifted, to have turned about. One defines him, yet he will not stay defined. No label ever covers him.

Rabbi Nachman is not a comfort as a leader. He lived a life that he compared to the moon, a life of constant struggle and spiritual growth, closeness and distance. So does a person who connects to the path of Rabbi Nachman feel that he also must constantly struggle and grow, sometimes close, sometimes distant.

Even in Rabbi Nachman's day, he attracted both great spiritual personalities and people who were imbalanced. Once, someone questioned Rabbi Nachman about this, and he replied that one cannot fault his teachings for the state such people are in, just as one would not fault a great doctor because he attracts unhealthy people.

But can Rabbi Nachman's teachings and path, without the influence of a balanced, personal teacher, help people who come to them out of a state of personal imbalance? One hears of people who come to Rabbi Nachman's teachings for a cure and are not helped, or whose problems are exacerbated. A person who feels alienated from others can have that heightened by practicing *hitbodedut*, isolated, spontaneous prayer. A person

Yet there is also a place for spirituality of a different phase: the spirituality of tranquillity.

For almost two hundred years, elders have been dissuading young people from proceeding onto the path of Bratslav. In Rabbi Kook we have an elder who himself appreciates the greatness of Rabbi Nachman. Precisely such a man, one who has studied Rabbi Nachman, examined his path critically and remained with it, and who is, furthermore, great in his own right, has the authority to offer cautionary words.

Rabbi Kook seems to be saying that in studying Bratslav Chasidism, we are studying the internal makeup of Rabbi Nachman's soul. Rabbi Nachman himself asserted that in a person's Torah writings, one can see his face. But, says Rabbi Kook, one cannot go to Rabbi Nachman expecting to receive from him all one's spiritual and emotional nourishment. As the rabbis said, "Beware of the coals of the rabbis so that you do not get burned; their bite is the bite of a fox, and their sting is the sting of a scorpion" (Ethics of the Fathers, 2:15). One would be equally ill-advised to enter the training room of a black belt aikido class without preparation and engage the sensei in combat. Even if the sensei has no wish to inflict injury, the nature of the meeting will likely lead to harm.

Rabbi Kook seems to be saying that Rabbi Nachman teaches holiness; however, he does not teach wholesomeness. But this does not mean that Rabbi Nachman is unwholesome. "The internal being of this great man needs much study."

Some enthusiasts feel that all they need are the teachings of Rabbi Nachman. Therefore, wholesomeness is irrelevant to them. Rabbi Kook points out that this is a mistake. One first needs to take healthy care of oneself, both psychologically and physically. Only then can one expose oneself to the heady world of Bratslav Chasidism. Bratslav Chasidism is the point of a needle. But one must first learn to walk securely on solid ground.

In the style and stress of his teachings, Rabbi Nachman's appreciation of the importance of being wellgrounded can be easily overlooked. For instance, there are many Bratslav teachings on extraordinary spiritual devotion, yet almost nothing is said about basic day-to-day spiritual life. Much is said about the follower's relation to the *tzaddik*; very little is taught about the role of camaraderie and friendship. A great deal of stress is placed on learning Torah; comparatively little on teaching Torah to others. There is much emphasis on serving God through emotional arousal; much less on integrating such arousal into one's intellect.

One cannot necessarily infer that Rabbi Nachman felt that the subjects he stressed were more important than those he did not; merely that he felt that for his students, these needed more attention.

In general, Chasidism is not meant to serve as a teacher of emotional health. As Rabbi Yosef Yitzchak Schneersohn, the previous Lubavitcher rebbe, teaches, "Fixing one's personality traits has nothing to do with Chasidism. Correcting those traits has to come first."[3]

Rabbi Kook was deeply drawn after the teachings of Rabbi Nachman. People who knew him testified that he learned Rabbi Nachman's teachings intensively and viewed them as among the foundations of his own outlook.

More than that, Rabbi Kook once uttered the astonishing words, "I am the soul of Rabbi Nachman."[4]

Perhaps Rabbi Kook meant to say that he was developing the path that Rabbi Nachman had initiated. For the needs of a new era with a new consciousness, Rabbi Kook was teaching a new Torah path that was a natural development of Rabbi Nachman's teachings. Just as classical Jewish mysticism was nested in Rabbi Nachman and was made accessible in a heartfelt mode to all Jews, so was Rabbi Nachman nested in Rabbi Kook and made accessible by him in a holistic and integrative manner to all Jews.

It is interesting to note, in regard to this connection between Rabbi Nachman and Rabbi Kook, that Rabbi Nachman claimed that he reached a qualitatively higher level upon his visit to the Land of Israel. Rabbi Kook too seems to have gone through a similar change (this pointed out by Rabbi Bezalel Naor). Also,

---

3. Yosef Yitzchak Schneersohn, *Likkutei Dibburim* (Brooklyn, NY: Otsar Hasefarim, 1980), p. 393.

4. *Chayei Harayeh*, p. 171.

Rabbi Kook came to Israel when he was 39 years old, which is one year older than Rabbi Nachman was when he passed away. This seems emblematic of Rabbi Kook's continuing and developing the path of Rabbi Nachman.

IV. One can also approach the puzzle of Rabbi Nachman's teachings in the following manner:

In Jewish thought (in particular, as expressed in the *Tanya*), every individual has both an animal and a Godly soul. The animal soul is a person's eros, his vital self. It includes all of his daily attributes: his desires, his emotions, his psychological makeup, and much of his spiritual feelings. The vast majority of people identify with their animal soul. Only the very rare *tzaddik* identifies with his Godly soul, seeing things from a radically spiritual perspective.

Rabbi Nachman at times deals with people trapped in physicality not by focusing on correcting their animal soul, but by shocking them with a consciousness that is identified with the Godly soul. He is trying to knock them into a totally different state of consciousness, just as the Jews left Egypt "in great haste."

Rabbi Nachman's teachings then seem designed to switch people trapped in physicality into a sudden identification with their Godly soul. This can result in a sudden rush of ecstasy and spiritual fervor.

However, there are two dangers extant. The first is that ultimately a person with problems on his level of daily consciousness cannot abandon them. He must return to his daily level and solve those problems — as Rabbi Nachman himself points out in several teachings.

Second, teachings that are apropos from the point of view of a man who identifies with his Godly soul can be unhealthy for those who identify with their animal soul — especially for those who are not psychologically healthy.

The most egregious example is Rabbi Nachman's series of negative statements related to sexuality. A man who identifies with his Godly soul will see how physical desire tends to pull him away from that self-identification. But for a person who identifies with his animal soul, such statements can reinforce negative and repressive attitudes toward his sexuality.

Also, in dealing with Rabbi Nachman, one must raise the question of cultural context.

Rabbi Nachman was speaking to simple *chasidim* living in small towns in the Ukraine, brought up in a spirit of intense and unsophisticated faith, and beginning to be exposed to the ideas of science and the Enlightenment through the medium of followers of the *Haskalah*, whose program was to minimize the Jews' obeisance to the Torah and to uproot their non-intellectual piety. These people had no contact whatsoever with science and culture beyond Torah. And the science of that day was being used as a tool with which to fight religion.

We today, however, are thoroughly immersed in a great deal of cultural sophistication. Once the genie is out of the bottle, one cannot simply stuff it back in. What is good for one set of circumstances is inappropriate for another.

For instance, Rabbi Nachman stressed the great importance of avoiding philosophical thinking and even forbade his followers to learn the philosophical works of leading Torah personalities. He stressed simple faith in the Torah and the *tzaddik*. He disparaged science and forbade his followers any kind of secular learning.

The person approaching Bratslav Chasidism must do so with a lively sense of what is good for him.

It is a standard refrain in Bratslav literature that Rabbi Nachman's words about a given subject cannot be adequately transcribed. Rabbi Nachman's teachings as applied to all possible situations have not been recorded. One must take the teachings that have been recorded and attempt, with intelligence and sensitivity, to apply them to one's own life, modifying them where one finds it necessary. Within a broad framework of *halachah* (Jewish law and practice), one applies spiritual teachings insofar as they develop one's health and enhance one's well-being.

Rabbi Nachman gave guidelines to lead people to liberation. Rabbi Nachman's teachings may be used as powerful tools to inspire one and to advance one's individualistic spiritual growth.

Selections in this anthology draw upon various works, some written by Rabbi Nachman himself and some by his leading follower and Boswell, Rabbi Nosson. Thus, some selections present Rabbi Nachman's teachings outright, and others are written in the third person – e.g., "Rabbi Nachman said."

Selections from Rabbi Nachman's magnum opus, *Likkutei Moharan*, are in general short excerpts. This is because the original teachings are often extremely compressed, presenting several intersecting ideas simultaneously, and expressed in a telegraphic style that is heavily weighted with associative word play. Such teachings are difficult in the original and much more so in English translation. But more than this, to really understand these teachings in their depth, one needs great expertise in kabbalistic texts and the ability to link those to psychological models. This is beyond my abilities and not the purpose of this volume. The purpose of this book is simply to share with the reader my own personal and perhaps idiosyncratic appreciation of Rabbi Nachman's teachings in the arenas of inspiration, enlightening concepts, and poetic literature.

Rabbi Nachman also told evocative stories and reported on mystical experiences. These too often are complex and multi-textured. In this anthology, they have been placed under various headings, but at times, this has been somewhat arbitrary.

1

The Essential Self

The Prince Who Thought
He Was a Turkey

Once there was a prince who had the delusion that he was a turkey. He sat naked underneath a table and pecked at bones and pieces of bread.

All the doctors despaired of healing him, and the king was very sad.

Then a wise man came and said, "I will try to heal him."

The wise man took off his clothes and sat under the table next to the prince, and he also pecked at crumbs and bones.

The prince asked him, "Who are you? What are you doing here?"

The wise man answered, "And what are you doing here?"

"I am a rooster."

"I am also a rooster."

The two of them sat there for some time until they got used to each other.

Then the wise man gave a signal, and a shirt was thrown down.

The wise man said to the prince, "Do you think that a rooster cannot wear a shirt? One can wear a shirt and still be a rooster."

So both of them put on shirts.

After a while, he signaled again, and a pair of trousers was thrown down to him.

He said, "Do you think that if someone wears pants, he cannot be a rooster?"

This went on until they were both dressed.

Afterward, he signaled and human food was thrown down from the table. He said to the prince, "Do you think that if you eat good food, you're no longer a turkey? One can eat and still be a turkey." So they both ate.

After that, he told the prince, "Do you think that a turkey can only sit under the table? One can sit at the table and still be a turkey."

And he continued to act in this way until he completely cured the prince.[1]

⋘

True Humility

People are very mistaken about what humility is.

We expend so much energy serving God and praying in order to go from small-mindedness to an expanded consciousness.

It isn't possible that we are supposed to be humble according to the simple meaning of the word, because that would require us to remain small-minded.

This matter must be approached with understanding. Not everyone can be truly humble. Only Moses was "more humble than any other man upon the earth" (Numbers 12:3).

Our sages called imperfect humility sycophancy. When Hannaniah, a false prophet, predicted that God would soon redeem the Jews, Jeremiah humbly added, "Amen, so may God do" (Jeremiah 28:6). Our sages said in regard to this episode that

---

1. Source: *Kochavei Ohr* (Jerusalem: Hasidei Breslov, 5732), p. 26.

"whoever praises another hypocritically ultimately falls into his hands—and if not into his hands, into the hands of his son" (*Sotah* 41b).[2]

❮❮❮

Belief in Oneself

Rabbi Nachman told me (Rabbi Nosson) that when a person is small in faith, it is difficult for him to serve God.

I stood before him in shock, [assuming I was being rebuked,] and I was very upset. It appeared to me that I do have at least some faith.

Rabbi Nachman chided me, "Some?"—as though to say, "And if you do have faith, you don't have faith in yourself."

He immediately mentioned the statement in the Talmud, "Who is responsible that the table of *tzaddikim* should be despised in the future days? The smallness that was in them"—that is, they didn't believe in themselves (*Sotah* 48b).

Rashi explains this to mean smallness of faith in God. But the actual language of the Talmud is "the smallness that was in them." It seems that one can interpret Rabbi Nachman's words to mean that they didn't believe that God is good to all and so that they themselves are important in His eyes. This caused them to be small. This was their smallness of faith: they didn't believe in themselves. (One can also interpret Rashi's words to be referring to lack of faith in themselves.)

One can understand from Rabbi Nachman's statement that a person must have faith that God loves him too. Because of God's great goodness, God considers him important too.

Being small-minded is not humility. One must pray a great deal to attain true humility.

Soon after this, Rabbi Nachman taught that some people are

---

2. As a result of this mistaken humility—for he should have explicitly refuted the false prophecy—Jeremiah suffered imprisonment.

Source: *Likkutei Moharan* (Jerusalem: Meshech Hanachal, 5750), 1:2:22.

the subject of controversy because they do not have faith in themselves.[3]

❀❀❀

May It Be My Will

Rabbi Nachman said that a person must come to such a degree of self-nullification that he can say, "May it be my will" [rather than "May it be Your will"]. (This is the level of the Torah of God and the prayer of God—see Chapter 36, this volume.)[4]

❀❀❀

God Does Not Need to Serve Himself

Rabbi Nachman said, "I can make all of you complete, awesome *tzaddikim*, but what of that? It would be like God serving Himself." He wanted that we ourselves should strive, using his strength and holy advice on how to serve God—not that he should give everything over to us completely.

Rabbi Nachman once told me, "If God wanted to serve Himself, He wouldn't need you." [5]

❀❀❀

To Find the Hidden Good

A person has to judge everyone favorably. Even if someone is completely bad, one must search for even a little bit of good in him. In that little bit of goodness, that person isn't bad.

---

3. Source: *Sichot Haran*, no. 140.

4. Source: *Avanehah Barzel* (Jerusalem: Hasidei Breslov, 5732), p. 44.

5. Source: *Chayei Moharan* (Brooklyn: Hasidei Breslov, 5734), part 1, p. 21, no. 40.

As a result of finding this little bit of good in the person and judging him favorably, one actually raises him up, and one can cause him to repent.

This is related to the verse, "A little more and there is no wicked person; You will look upon his place, and he is not there" (Psalms 37:10).

This verse exhorts us to judge everyone favorably. Even though you see that someone is completely bad, you must find some little bit of good in him where he isn't evil. This is what the verse means when it says, "A little more and there is no wicked person." You must find that little more of goodness that he still has, where he isn't bad. Even if he is bad, how is it possible that he doesn't even have a little bit of good? How could it be that he never did a *mitzvah* or some good deed in his life? By finding some small area of goodness where he isn't bad and judging him favorably, you raise him from the side of guilt to the side of merit, until he repents.

As a result of finding a little good where he isn't wicked, then "you will look upon his place and he is not there." When you look upon his place, his level, you will see that he is no longer there; by finding some little bit of good in him and judging him favorably, one moves him from the side of guilt to the side of merit.

Understand this.

One must also apply this technique to oneself. A person has to work hard to be constantly joyful and to keep from being depressed.

Even if, when a person begins to look at himself, he sees that he has no good in himself and that he is full of wrongdoing; even if the Evil One wants to cast him into depression—he must not allow himself to fall! Instead, he must search and find in himself some little bit of good. How could it be that he never once did a *mitzvah* or some good deed?

It is possible that, looking into that good deed, one will see that it was imperfect, full of flaws and ulterior motives. Nevertheless, how is it possible that it didn't contain some little good? At the very least, there was some point of goodness in what one did.

One must find that little bit of good in oneself and use it to revivify oneself and become joyful.

Then one moves from the side of guilt to the side of merit, and one can repent.

One must judge oneself favorably; one must strengthen oneself so that one won't fall completely. One must revivify oneself and make oneself joyful with the little bit of good one finds within oneself, with the fact that one managed to do some *mitzvah* or good deed.

After one has done that, one must search yet more and find some other bit of good. Even though that bit of good is also mixed with a great deal of waste, one must draw out the good point.

One must search for and gather all the good points.

In this way, one makes spiritual melodies with one's soul, like a musician who plucks out the notes that comprise a melody.[6]

❦❦❦

Bringing Forth the Good

Once, Rabbi Gershon of Tirhavtzia complained at length to Rabbi Nachman that he was having trouble serving God.

Rabbi Nachman replied, "For the present, do good and serve God honestly. When you serve God like this constantly, the good will remain and the bad will fall away of itself."[7]

---

6. Source: *Likkutei Moharan* 1:282.
7. Source: *Chayei Moharan* 2:49, no. 4.

2

Coming to God

Expertise on All Levels

When a person wishes to return [to God], he must be an expert in *halachah* (literally, "going" – Jewish law). He must have two types of expertise: expertise in running out and expertise in returning. As the Zohar says in a parallel image, "Fortunate is he who enters and comes out" (*Vayechel* 213b; *Haazinu* 282a).

"If I go up to heaven, You are there" (Psalms 139:8). This is the level of entering, of running. "And if I spread out my couch in Sheol, you are there." That is the level of coming out, of returning.

This is related to the verse, "I am my beloved's and my beloved is mine" (Song of Songs 6:3). "I am my beloved's" is the level of entering. "And my beloved is mine" is the level of coming out. This is the essence of God's glory.

This is related to the verse, "Honor Him by not going on your [daily] ways" (Isaiah 58:18). "Your ways" is plural, referring to both entering in and coming out.

When a person has these two types of expertise, he can return [to God]. He attains God's honor, as in the verse, "Honor Him by

7

not going on your [daily] ways," which can be literally read as "Honor Him in the action of your ways."

One then attains the crown. . . . Then God's hand is outstretched to accept one's return.

When a person wishes to return [to God,] he must have these two types of expertise: expertise in running and in returning, in entering and coming out: the level of "if I go up to heaven, there you are," expertise in running, "and if I spread my couch in Sheol, You are there," expertise in returning.

When a person wants to return to God, he must gird his loins and strengthen himself in the ways of God continuously.

When he is rising, that is the level of "If I rise to heaven . . . and spread out my couch." If he has attained a high level, he should not remain there contentedly, but with great expertise he should know and believe that he must go farther. This is the level of being an expert in running, in entering–the level of "if I go up to heaven."

Contrarily, if he falls, even to the depths of Sheol, he should not despair. He should constantly search for God and strengthen himself in every way with anything that he can, for God is also found in the depths of hell. There too one can cling to Him. This is the level of "If I spread out my couch in Sheol, You are there." This is the level of expertise in returning.

It is impossible to come close to God without being an expert in these two areas.

Rabbi Nachman was very precise and called this matter expertise. It is a very great expertise to know how to toil and work in serving God constantly, and at every moment to seek to come to a higher level without falling.

Even if bad things have happened, a person should still not be discouraged. He should live the meaning of the verse, "If I spread out my couch in Sheol, You are there."[1]

᭢᭢᭢

---

1. Source: *Likkutei Moharan* 1:6:4.

Repentance Is Higher than the Torah

Rabbi Nachman lavishly praised the power of repentance. Even if a person has fallen very low, it is forbidden to despair. Repentance is even higher than the Torah. Therefore, there is no despair in the world. One's sins can turn into something else entirely. As our sages said, "Sins can be turned into merits" (*Yoma* 86b). This matter contains mystic secrets.

One can easily return to God from any descents, because God's greatness has no end. One must simply never give up crying out to God, pleading and praying to Him constantly.[2]

€€€

If You Only Hope

Rabbi Nachman once quoted the verse, "Be strong and mighty, all those who hope for God" (Psalms 31:25). "All those who hope"—even if you have not reached any level of holiness, but you only hope, still, "be strong and mighty" and do not let anything in the world upset you.[3]

---

2. Source: *Sichot Haran*, no. 3.
3. Source: *Sichot Haran*, no. 120.

3

Self-Improvement

If You Believe That You Can Ruin. . .

Regarding not allowing oneself to fall no matter how imperfect one's past has been, Rabbi Nachman said, "If you believe that you are able to ruin things, then believe that you are able to fix them."[1]

❦❦❦

The Constant Leap

Rabbi Nachman said to someone who was about to get married, "How does one dance before the bride?" He was hinting to him, "How does one dance and leap beyond the level one was previously on?"[2]

---

1. Source: *Likkutei Moharan* 2:112.
2. Source: *Chayei Moharan* 2:70, no. 134.

11

€€€

Speech of the Broken Heart

One of Rabbi Nachman's followers once asked him the difference
between a broken heart and depression.

Rabbi Nachman replied that a broken heart means that even
when one is standing among others, one can turn one's face aside
and call out to God. At that point, Rabbi Nachman exclaimed,
"Master of the world," raising his hands with great longing.[3]

€€€

Constant Self-Renewal

Rabbi Nachman spoke at length of the great awe, holiness, and
quickness that he had had as a child.

He said that he would start many times in one day. He would
resolve to be a good person from this moment on and serve God.
On the same day, he would fall prey to lust for food and the like.
He would again resolve that from that moment on, he would be
a good person. And he would fall again, and again begin afresh.
This happened many times in one day.

He had many beginnings. Every day he began anew to serve
God.

This is a great principle in serving God: one should not allow
oneself to fall because one sinned or fell from some level of
devotion of serving God.

One must strengthen oneself and begin anew, as though one is
beginning for the first time.

Even if this occurs many times, one should begin anew.

Without this practice, one cannot really be a kosher person
and come close to God.

One must be strong in one's intent to come close to God, even
if one is falling. One must still yearn for God, cry out, pray, and

---

3. Source: *Sichot Haran*, no. 231.

do whatever one must to serve God joyfully. Without this attitude, one cannot really come close to God.

One must resolve that one would be satisfied to serve God one's entire life without receiving any reward.

It may appear that one is so far from God that one is unlikely to receive the reward of the world-to-come. Even so, one must be satisfied to do whatever one can to serve God, even without the world-to-come.

Even if it appears that one will go to hell, one is still obligated to do what one must to serve God as much as one can – to grab every opportunity to do a *mitzvah*, learn Torah, or pray. Then God will do what is right in His eyes.

Once, the Baal Shem Tov grew very despondent, to the point that he imagined that he would not have the world-to-come. He had nothing with which to enliven himself. He declared, "If this is the case, I will love God without the world-to-come." Similarly, every person, even a simple person, can only become kosher when he withstands everything. Even in a single day, he may have to strengthen himself many times and continuously begin afresh, until he finally manages to go in the way of God.[4]

❦❦❦

The Concealed Reward

I heard that Rabbi Nachman told a very accomplished person, a good and God-fearing man, that God doesn't show some people what they accomplished until after they die.

I understood that Rabbi Nachman meant to encourage him even though he may not see any results of his service.[5]

❦❦❦

Ashes

Rabbi Nachman told Rabbi Nosson of a great *tzaddik* who at times told himself that even if he will become ashes beneath the

---

4. Source: *Sichot Haran*, no. 48.
5. Source: *Sichot Haran*, no. 244.

feet of the *tzaddikim*, as our sages described the fate of souls of evil people, he will, at any rate, not be a complete nothing.

Rabbi Nachman told this to encourage me: even such a great *tzaddik* grew so discouraged, to the point that he imagined that the most he could hope for was that he would at least not become an absolute nothing.

Our sages said that a person could become ashes, but this ash would still have some vitality; and that too is good, for at least it isn't nothing.

It seems from Rabbi Nachman's words that he encouraged himself this way a number of times. He comforted himself that if this would occur, he would at any rate be reconciled to serve God in whatever way he can for the rest of his life.[6]

⋘

The Rejected *Tzaddik*

In *Kislev* of 5570 (1809), here in Bratslav, I had a dream that I was sitting in a room of my small building adjacent to the house. No one came to see me, and I was very surprised. I went to the other room, but there was no one there either. I went into the house and then into the *beis medrash*, but there was no one there either.

I decided to go out. When I went outside, I saw people standing there in circles, whispering with each other. One made fun of me, another laughed at me, another looked at me arrogantly, and so forth. Even my followers were against me. A few acted arrogantly, a few whispered secretly about me, and the like.

I called one of my followers and asked him, "What is going on?"

He replied, "How could you do such a thing? Is it possible that you should commit such a great sin?"

I had no idea why they were mocking me. I asked this man to

---

6. Source: *Chayei Moharan* 2:73, no. 142.

bring together all my followers. He left me, and I didn't see him again.

I sat alone, trying to decide what to do. Finally, I decided to travel to another country.

But when I got there, the people were standing about and speaking of this matter. Even there, they knew of the matter.

I decided to go live in a forest. Five of my followers joined me, and together we went to the forest. We lived there, and whenever we needed anything, such as food and the like, one of them would go and buy what we needed. I would always ask him if the commotion had died down, and he would always reply, "No, it is still very strong."

While we were living there, an old man came to me. He said that he had something to talk about with me.

I went with him, and he began to speak with me.

He said, "Did you do such a thing? How can you not be ashamed before your elders — before your grandfather, Rabbi Nachman and before your great-grandfather, the Baal Shem Tov? How can you not be ashamed before the Torah of Moses and before our holy forefathers, Abraham, Isaac, and Jacob, and the others? Do you think that you will live here forever? Won't your money run out? And you are a weak person. What will you do?

"Do you think that you will go to another country? What good will it do? If they don't know who you are, you won't be able to stay there because they won't give you money. And if they do know who you are, you won't be able to live there because they will know about this."

I answered him, "Since this is so and I must keep running, at least I have the world-to-come."

He replied, "Do you think you have the world-to-come? You committed such a desecration of God's name that you won't even have a place to hide in Gehinnom."

I replied, "Go away from me. I thought that you would comfort me, but you are causing me to suffer. Go away."

The old man left me.

As I sat there, I decided that since I am staying here for such a long time, I may forget my learning entirely. I told one of the

men that when he went to the city he should look for a book and
bring it back with him.

He went to the city but he returned without a book. He said
that it was an impossible task. He could not tell who the book
was for, of course; and it was impossible to take it secretly.

I suffered very much: first, because I was wandering about,
and now, because I didn't have a book and I might forget my
learning entirely.

A while later, the old man returned, carrying a book under his
arm.

I asked him, "What are you carrying?"

"A book."

"Give it to me."

He gave me the book. When I took it, I didn't even know how
to hold it. And when I opened it, I didn't have any idea what was
in it. It was as though it was in a foreign language and a foreign
script. This caused me a great deal of suffering. I was afraid that
if my followers found out about this, they would leave me.

The old man again called me over to speak with me. I went
with him, and he again began to tell me, "How could you have
done such a thing? How can you not be ashamed? You won't
even have a place to hide in *Gehinnom*."

I told him, "If a man from the upper world would tell me such
a thing, I would believe him."

He answered, "I am from there"; and he gave me a sign from
there.

I recalled the well-known story of the Baal Shem Tov. The
Baal Shem Tov had once thought that he had no portion in the
world-to-come, and he said, "I love God without the world-to-
come."

I threw my head back with very great bitterness. When I
threw my head back, all the people before whom the old man
said I should be ashamed came to me—my grandfather, the
forefathers, and so forth. They quoted the verse to me, "The fruit
of the land will be for glory and for beauty" (Isaiah 4:2). They
told me, "Now we will take pride in you."

They brought me all my followers and children (because at
first even my own children had left me), and they consoled me.

As for how I threw my head back – even if a person had sinned eight hundred times against the entire Torah, if he were to throw his head back with such bitterness, he would certainly be forgiven.

As for the rest of the good, I do not want to tell you. But it was certainly good.[7]

7. Source: *Chayei Moharan* 1:42, no. 11.

4

Being Balanced

Fanaticism

One does not need to be a fanatic.

When a person throws off all the concerns of this world and only works to serve God, he is considered a fanatic. I myself do not regard such behavior as fanaticism. To the contrary, it is when a person runs after the things of this world and is far from serving God that he is really a fanatic.

Nevertheless, even what the world calls fanaticism is unnecessary. One can be a kosher person without fanaticism.[1]

€€€

Leniency

At the time of the fires here in Bratslav – once on Shabbat and once on Yom Kippur – Rabbi Nachman wanted us to be very lenient regarding the laws of Shabbat and Yom Kippur in order

---

1. Source: *Sichot Haran*, no. 51.

to save our money (it is clear that he meant in a way that is halachically permissible). After Yom Kippur, he said that there are a number of lenient responsa that allow one a great deal of latitude.

He said, "There are some people who for the sake of one stringency wipe out a great deal of their service of God, sometimes almost all of it. How hard does a person work to make a living, traveling on the road without a chance of learning Torah, praying or serving God for many days? Then, for the sake of one stringency, he can lose it all, God forbid, and he has to start all over again."[2]

❮❮❮

Passover Stringencies

Rabbi Nachman admonished people not to be overly stringent, for "God is not unfair" (*Avodah Zarah* 3a), and "The Torah was not given to angels" (*Berachot* 25b).

Every person should pick one *mitzvah* that he will fulfill as best as he can with all its stringencies. But even there, he should not do foolish things that will lead him to depression.

As for the rest of the *mitzvot*, however, one does not have to be overly stringent. One should just work to keep all of the Torah's *mitzvot* simply.

In particular, this holds true for the stringencies of Passover, above and beyond the halachic requirements. Rabbi Nachman did not at all agree with those who were overzealous, which led them to become depressed.

One of Rabbi Nachman's followers asked him about what to do in regard to a particular Passover stringency.

Rabbi Nachman made fun of this. He spoke at length on the theme that one does not have to search after stringencies that drive one crazy.

He said that he himself used to invent all sorts of stringencies. One year, he was afraid that the water he would use on Passover might contain some leaven. Some people stored water for

---

2. Source: *Chayei Moharan* 2:65, no. 100.

Passover. But he was afraid that this water might also get leaven in it. He decided that he would only use flowing spring water. But there was no spring where he lived, so he considered going off to a place with a spring and spending Passover there.

To such a degree was he taken up with unnecessary stringencies.

But now, he said, he laughs at this. Beyond keeping the basic *halachah*, one does not need to search after stringencies, even on Passover.

The essence of serving God is simplicity: learning a great deal, praying a great deal, and doing good deeds. The Torah was not given to angels. One does not have to be overstrict with oneself. One simply does what one can.[3]

€€€

Don't Begin to Think at All

Once, I (Rabbi Nosson) told Rabbi Nachman about the many thoughts that confused and depressed me when I would do a *mitzvah* such as washing my hands, and I became filled with all sorts of worries that I hadn't done the *mitzvah* properly.

Rabbi Nachman replied, "I already spoke with you that you don't have to pay any attention to this."

But I told Rabbi Nachman that [my knowledge of this] itself confused me.

Rabbi Nachman replied, "Then don't begin to think at all."[4]

€€€

Step by Step

A person must serve God at every moment. The essence is action: to learn a great deal; to do many *mitzvot*; to pray a great deal, pouring one's heart out before God; and so on.

---

3. Source: *Sichot Haran*, no. 235.
4. Source: *Chayei Moharan* 2:58, no. 60.

A person should not get overwhelmed when he reads about the many types of service that the holy books discuss. He shouldn't ask, "When will I be able to do even one of these things, much less all of them?"

He must not be impatient and try to do everything at once. He should proceed at a comfortable pace, one level after the next. He should not be overwhelmed and confused, trying to do everything at once.

This is similar to a fire breaking out, God forbid. In their panic, people grab what they don't need.

A person should go step by step. In addition, if at times he is unable to do anything in serving God, what of it? The Talmud teaches that "the Compassionate One forgives a person who is under duress" (*Bava Kama* 28b).

He should accustom himself to yearn greatly at all times for God. Such yearning is itself a very great thing. As the Talmud states, "The Compassionate One desires the heart."

We heard a number of talks and stories regarding this topic. But it is not possible to explain these things well in writing. The wise person who seeks truth will understand some of this.[5]

5. Source: *Sichot Haran*, no. 27.

5

Simplicity

Desire and Simplicity

I don't know who can say that he is serving God in accordance with God's greatness. If a person knows even a little bit of God's greatness, I don't know how he can say that he will serve God.

No angel or seraph can boast that it can serve God.

But one must always strongly desire to come close to God.

Even though everyone may desire to serve God, not all desires are equal. There are many gradations. Even a single person's desires have many gradations from moment to moment.

In the midst of this desire, one prays, one learns Torah and does *mitzvot*. (In relation to God's greatness, all this service is nothing. But one acts as if one is truly serving Him, even though this is almost comical in relation to God's greatness.)

One does not need to be clever. One merely needs simplicity.

But even in simplicity, one may not be a fool.

Still and all, one doesn't need to be clever at all.[1]

---

1. Source: *Sichot Haran*, no. 51.

23

€€€

The King and the Peasant

A king went out to catch animals. He traveled dressed like a
simple man so that he would be able to hunt easily. Suddenly, a
great rain cascaded down on him. All the ministers were scattered, and the king himself was in great danger. He finally came
across a peasant's house. The peasant took in the king, clothed
him, gave him groats to eat, heated the oven up for him, gave
him a place to sleep on the pallet, and so on.

The king was terribly worn out, and he had never felt anything
as warm and sweet as the peasant's care for him.

The ministers searched for the king until they came to the
peasant's house and saw him sleeping. They wanted the king to
return with them to the palace.

The king replied to them, "You all ran off to save yourselves,
and you didn't save me. Yet this man saved me, and I had such
a wonderful experience here. Therefore, he will bring me back
to the palace in his wagon and in these clothes, and he will put
me on my throne."

Rabbi Nachman added, "In the days before the coming of the
messiah, there will be a flood of heresy, a flood of destructive
waters. The highest mountains will be covered, and the flood
will even dash its waters over the land of Israel. The water will
even spray into kosher hearts; and through sophistication, no
one will find an answer.

"All the ministers will scatter, and the kingdom will not
remain firm. It will stand only because of simple Jews who recite
psalms and serve God simply.

"Therefore, when the messiah comes, it is the simple people
who will place the crown upon his head."[2]

€€€

---

2. Source: *Avanehah Barzel*, p. 23.

The Simplicity of God

One does not need cleverness to serve God – just simplicity and faith.

Rabbi Nachman said that simplicity is the highest level. God Himself is higher than everything, and He is the ultimately simple being.[3]

≪≪≪

The Holy Fool

It is better to be a "fool who believes everything" (Proverbs 14:15) – that is, to believe even foolish things and lies – in order that one also believes the truth, than to be clever and deny everything. When one looks at everything as a joke, one even denies the truth. "It is better that I should be called a fool all the days of my life than be evil even one hour before God" (*Eduyot* 5:6).[4]

≪≪≪

The Cry from the Heart

The cry from the heart is itself faith. Even if a person has many doubts, when he cries out, his heart still has a spark of holy faith. If not, he would not cry out. So the cry itself is on the level of faith.

From the outcry, one comes to faith. Although the outcry is on the level of faith, this faith is very small. When one cries out, one can enlarge the faith, until one's questions fall away. But even if one does not reach that level, crying out is still a very good thing.[5]

---

3. Source: *Sichot Haran*, no. 101.
4. Source: *Sichot Haran*, no. 103.
5. Source: *Sichot Haran*, no. 146.

❮❮❮

The Clever Man and the Simple Man

Once, when the king was going through the census records, he saw the names of one man called Clever and another called Simple.

The king was intrigued by these names.

He very much wanted to meet these people. It occurred to him that if he summoned them suddenly, they would be very frightened. The clever man wouldn't know how to answer him, and the simple man might go mad from fright.

So the king decided that he would send a clever messenger to the clever man and a simple messenger to the simple man. . . .

He gave each messenger a letter.

He also gave them letters for the governor of the state where the two men lived. The king instructed the governor to send letters in his own name to the clever man and the simple man so that they would not become frightened. The governor should write them that the matter is not urgent. The king has not commanded them to come to him – they themselves can decide what to do – but the king would like to meet them.

The clever and the simple messengers came to the governor and gave him the letter.

The governor inquired about these two people.

He was told that the clever man was incredibly brilliant and very wealthy. And the simple man was very simple, with one rough fur coat that he treated as though it was an entire wardrobe of garments.

The governor decided that it would not be right to bring the simple man to the king in such a fur coat. He made him good clothing and placed them in the simple messenger's carriage. Then he gave both messengers the letters.

The messengers went and delivered their letters. The clever messenger gave his letter to the clever man and the simple messenger gave his letter to the simple man.

When the simple man received his letter, he told the messenger, "I don't know what the letter says. Read it to me."

The messenger replied, "I can tell it to you by heart. The king wants you to come to him right away."

The simple man asked, "You aren't making fun of me?"

"Not at all. It's really true, without any jokes."

The simple man was filled with joy. He ran to his wife and told her, "My wife, the king has sent for me."

She asked him, "What's going on? Why did he send for you?"

But he had no time to answer. He quickly and joyfully hurried into the carriage to travel with the messenger.

Then, when he saw the clothing, he was even happier than before – on top of everything, he has clothes!

And he was very happy. . . .

Meanwhile, when the clever messenger gave his letter to the clever man, the clever man said, "Wait and stay here overnight. We'll talk and decide what to do."

That night, the clever man prepared a feast for the messenger. As they ate, the clever man began thinking aloud, using his cleverness and his philosophical training. "What can this mean? What kind of king would send for such an insignificant person like me? Who am I that the king should send for me? Such a great king who has such a great government? Should I say that he sent for me because of my cleverness? But he must have clever people around him, and he himself must be very clever. So why should he send for me?"

He thought this over a great deal. And as he pondered, he finally turned to the messenger and said, "Do you know what I think? It is clear that there is no king in the world. The whole world has made a mistake when they think there is a king.

"It's patently ridiculous. How could it be that the entire world would allow itself to be ruled by one man? Obviously, there isn't any king who rules the world."

The clever messenger protested, "But I brought you a letter from the king."

The clever man asked him, "Did you yourself take the letter from the king's hand?"

He replied, "No. Someone else delivered the letter to me."

"That proves my point! Examine this closely and you will see that I am right: there is no king."

The clever man asked the messenger further, "Tell me, you grew up in the royal city. Did you ever see the king?"

"No." (Indeed, not everyone gets to see the king, because the king only appears on rare occasions.)

"Now you see that I am right and that there is obviously no king. You yourself never even saw him."

The clever messenger asked, "If that's so, who is running the country?"

The clever man replied, "I will tell you. I am a hundred per cent sure about this. I traveled through many lands, including Italy. There, the custom is that there are seventy leaders who lead the land for a while, everyone taking a turn."

The clever man's words began to persuade the messenger, until they both decided that there is obviously no king in the world.

The clever man said, "Wait until the morning, and I will again prove to you that there is no king."

In the morning, the clever man got up and woke up the clever messenger. He told him, "Come with me into the street, and I will show you how the whole world is mistaken, and that there is no king."

They went to the marketplace, where they saw a soldier. They asked him, "Whom do you serve?"

"The king."

"Did you ever see the king in your life?"

"No."

So the clever man said, "You see, can there be greater foolishness than this?"[6]

_____

6. Source: *Sippurei Maasiyot*, "The Clever Man and the Simple Man," p. 72.

6

Despair Does Not Exist

Efficient Calm

If a person cannot fall asleep, he should not force himself. The more he forces himself, the more will he arouse whatever it is that is preventing him from falling asleep.

This holds true for all things: one should not force oneself too much. The more one forces oneself to do something, the more does one arouse opposition.

Even in serving God, one must at times not force oneself too much. Nevertheless, one must be vigorous in sanctifying oneself and acting well and quickly.

It is forbidden to put off till tomorrow what one can do today, for the world does not stand still for even the blink of an eye.

If possible, one should do whatever one can in serving God immediately, without even a moment's delay. Who knows how many delays he will have another time? A person has only this moment.

Still, one sometimes sees that although he is trying to attain something, he is not succeeding. Then one must wait without

29

growing discouraged or confused. One must wait until one's time comes.

Rabbi Nachman was unique in this matter. He was industrious without an equal. Whatever he had to do, even if it was a this-worldly matter, he would do immediately and quickly – and how much more if it was a matter of serving God.

Nevertheless, he was very calm. When he saw that something wasn't succeeding, he was very patient.

Even when one's service is not succeeding, one must continue to yearn for God constantly.

One must not despair of anything.

As soon as God helps one and one can attain some holy matter, one should do it immediately and with great enthusiasm.

This matter cannot be adequately described in print. The wise person who desires truth will understand a little from here how to serve God.[1]

€€€

Pressure

Rabbi Nachman said that when teachers pressure a child, the child doesn't learn anything at all.

One must skillfully teach the child bit by bit, without threats or pressure.

Then the child will grasp the material easily.

If the teacher reviews the material bit by bit, the child will understand and remember it. But if he keeps going over it and admonishing the child, "Remember! Remember!," when the child is asked the meaning of a verse, he might well answer that it means, "Remember!"

One should not pressure oneself overmuch regarding anything. One should proceed calmly, step by step.[2]

---

1. Source: *Chayei Moharan* 2:42, no. 2.
2. Source: *Chayei Moharan* 2:43, no. 3.

€€€

From the Depths

Rabbi Nachman said, "Even if a person has fallen to a low level, he must strengthen himself and not despair at all. God's greatness is much higher than the Torah; on God's level, everything can be rectified, for repentance is higher than Torah."

I asked him, "But how does one reach this?"

He answered, "One can reach this as long as one does not despair from crying out and praying. One should remain untiring until one finally succeeds."

This is because the essence of repentance is crying out to God.[3]

€€€

It Is Forbidden to Despair

It is forbidden to despair.

Even if a person is on the absolutely lowest level, even if he is in the depths of hell, he must not despair. He must emulate the verse, "From the belly of the depths have I called out" (Jonah 2:3). He must strengthen himself with whatever he can and believe that he too can return and receive life from the Torah via the *tzaddik*.

One must strengthen oneself to the greatest extent possible, for there is no despair in the world at all. (Rabbi Nachman said this in Yiddish: *Kein yiush is gar nit farhanden*; he drew out these words and said them forcefully and with great depth, to teach every individual for all generations never to despair, no matter what happens to him.) Whatever occurs, even if a person falls, when he strengthens himself on the level that he is on, he still has hope to return to God.[4]

---

3. Source: *Chayei Moharan* 2:67, no. 114.
4. Source: *Likkutei Moharan* 2:78.

7

Joy

Constantly Joyful

Rabbi Nachman spoke with me at length about joy. He encouraged me a great deal to be constantly joyful. He said, "When a sick person is lying in bed, people encourage him and tell him not to give up or get depressed. In that way, he can get well."[1]

€€€

The Melody of Joy

It is a very great *mitzvah* to be always joyful, and to push away depression with all one's strength.

All diseases are a result of a problem with joy.[2]

There are ten types of melody. And melody is associated with joy.

---

1. Source: *Chayei Moharan* 1:75, no. 17.
2. *Simchah*, joy, is a state of consciousness that puts one in touch with the healthy energy in the universe.

33

These two ideas are reflected in the verse, "On the ten-stringed instrument . . . You have given me joy with Your acts, O God" (Psalms 92:4–5).

When a person's joy, which corresponds to the ten categories of song, is incomplete, he grows ill. His corresponding ten pulses are harmed.

All diseases are included within the ten pulses.

Similarly, all melodies are included in these ten categories of song.

In accordance with a flaw in joy and melody, sickness comes.

When these ten categories of melody enter a person's ten different pulses, they revive him (*Tikkun* 69, 105a).

Doctors report that sickness is due to depression, and that joy is a vital healing agent.

In future days, joy will increase tremendously. Our sages state that in the future, "the Holy One, blessed be He, will be in the center of the circle of *tzaddikim*" (Jer. *Sukkah*, Chapter *Lulav V'aravah*; *Midrash Rabbah*, *Sh'mini*, 11:9).

God will make a circle of the *tzaddikim*, and He will be in their center.[3]

The sick person himself has no life force. Instead, God's presence gives him life.

In the future days, as a result of joy, illness will be rectified. Then God will be at the head of the sick person, for joy is associated with rectifying a sick person. That is why joy and dancing are both called *choleh*, for they both rectify illness.[4]

⋘

---

3. In the Hebrew, the word *center* is written literally as "at the head." Also, the word for circle, *choleh*, is homonymous with the word for a sick person. So we can understand this quote as related to the talmudic statement that God's presence hovers above the headboard of the sick person (*Nedarim* 40a).

4. Source: *Likkutei Moharan* 2:24.

The Task of Joy

A person must gather all his resources to be constantly happy.

As a result of day-to-day problems, human nature tends toward depression. Everyone has problems.

A person has to work very hard to force himself to be constantly joyful and to do whatever he can to make himself joyful—even with silly things.

It is true that a broken heart is very good. But that is only for a limited amount of time.

A person should set aside a certain amount of time every day to break his heart and speak to God in his own words. But for the rest of the day, he must be joyful.

It is much easier to shift from a broken heart to depression than it is to lose control as a result of joy.

So a person must be constantly joyful, except for a specific time when he has a broken heart.[5]

⋘

Joy and the *Tzaddik*

Rabbi Nachman once encouraged someone to be joyful. He said, "Be joyful in God. Even though you don't know God's greatness, you should rely on me, because I know God's greatness." He quoted the verse, "I know how great God is" (Psalms 135:5). He added, "You should also rejoice that you had a teacher like me."[6]

⋘

Joy through Everyday Life

Rabbi Nachman encouraged someone to be joyful even in general matters. He said to him, "At first you have to make

5. Source: *Likkutei Moharan* 2:24.
6. Source: *Sichot Haran*, no. 177.

yourself as happy as possible with everyday things. From that, you can come to true joy."[7]

❦❦❦

Accepting Everything with Joy

Rabbi Nachman left Bratslav soon after a fire had destroyed part of the town. He said, "It was right that I leave after this [fire]. It would not be right that while others are in sorrow, I am joyful. If [my house] had not been burned, I would have to join the others in their sorrow, because when a Jew has such a sorrow, I must take part.

"But now that my house was also burned, I must accept this in love and joy, and I need to be tremendously joyful. So it isn't right that I should be with the others; for how can I be joyful while they are full of sorrow?"

Understand this well.

Afterward, Rabbi Nachman said, "It goes without saying that I accept losing money with joy, since 'a person will exchange skin for skin, but he will give everything he has for his soul' (Job 2:4). Even if God were to take my life, God forbid, I would accept that with great joy too"—to such a point that he would have to force himself to cry and act sad, for he would be filled with such great joy. Everything was as one to him, as though he wasn't in the world at all.[8]

---

7. Source: *Sichot Haran*, no. 177.
8. Source: *Chayei Moharan* 1:76, no. 2.

8

Faith

The Greatness of Faith

Once, Rabbi Nachman was speaking about faith.

He said, "The world considers faith a small thing. But I consider faith a very great matter."

Faith must be without sophistication and philosophy, but with complete simplicity.[1]

❧❧❧

The World Was Created for Faith

I heard that Rabbi Nachman was once speaking with someone who had problems with faith. Rabbi Nachman told him, "God foresaw that there would be people who would have problems with their faith; doubts would arise in their minds, but they would struggle against those thoughts and strengthen their faith. Only for this did God create the entire universe."

---

1. Source: *Sichot Haran*, no. 33.

37

From then on, whenever this person was troubled by such thoughts, these words encouraged him greatly.

Rabbi Nachman's teachings also tell us that the universe was created in the merit of faith. As the verse says, "All His acts are faithful" (Psalms 33:4).[2]

◄◄◄

Holy Longing

Rabbi Nachman once praised the longing and desire for holy things. Even though one may not accomplish them, the longing itself is very good.[3]

---

2. Source: *Sichot Haran*, no. 222.
3. Source: *Sichot Haran*, no. 260.

9

Strife

The Root of Conflict

The entire world is filled with strife among nations and cities.

The same holds true within every house. Strife exists between neighbors, between a man and his wife, father and child, householder and servant, and so on.

No one takes to heart the end; every day people die. The day that passed no longer exists, and every day, a person draws closer to death.

It is all one: the strife between a man and his household is exactly the same as the strife between kings.

Every member of the family is like a separate nation; arguments are like wars between nations.

One can tell which type of nation each individual is. There are different types of nationalities: one is angry and murderous, and so on. One finds the same among family members.

Even if one person wants to live in harmony, he is forced to fight. We sometimes see that one nation desires to live in peace and would have been pleased to give way. But it is dragged into a war between two other parties, for each party declares it for its own, until both war against it.

A person is a little world. The entire world is within him. How much more is this true of a person and his household, in which are contained all the nations, warring against each other.

It sometimes happens that when a person lives alone in the forest, he goes insane. This is because he is alone: all the nations are contained within him; when they war against each other, he is forced to constantly change sides. He can go completely insane, because he keeps changing sides as the nations in him war against each other.

But when a person lives among others, there is room for the war to spread among the people in his house and his neighbors.

Also contained within a person are the wars between the tribes—Ephraim versus Judah, and the like.

When the messiah will come, all these controversies will come to an end, and there will be great peace in the world. As the verse teaches, "They will not do evil nor destroy" (Isaiah 11:9).[1]

⋘

The Regret of the Wicked

Wicked people are full of regret. But they have no idea what regret is.

The very fact that they act even more evil is itself regret. Because they have feelings of regret, they respond by acting yet more evil. This is like two men who are struggling with each other. When one sees that the other one is gaining over him, he summons up yet more strength to fight back. In the exact same way, when evil sees that some good is awakening in those people, it grows stronger.[2]

---

1. Source: *Sichot Haran*, no. 77.
2. Source: *Sichot Haran*, no. 10.

10

Chosen People

A Chosen People – Beyond Intellect

We are called "a singular – *segulah* – nation" (Deuteronomy 7:6). This is like a charm – *segulah* – used for healing. Even though nature does not necessitate that it heal, it does so in a manner that transcends nature and that human intellect cannot fathom.

Similarly, God took us to be a chosen people, even though human intellect cannot understand how God chose one nation from among the other nations. At the splitting of the Red Sea, the aspect of judgment complained, "Both nations are idol worshipers" (*Genesis Rabbah*, chap. 57, and *Exodus Rabbah*, chap 21). Nevertheless, God took us to be a holy nation.

This is like a charm, which is higher than nature and human intellect.[1]

❮❮❮

---

1. Source: *Likkutei Moharan* 1:29.

Transcending Ethics

Someone speaking with Rabbi Nachman praised a person who acted honestly, saying that he was *ehrintlech* – ethical.

Rabbi Nachman replied that the word *ethical* doesn't suffice to describe a Jew.

Non-Jews have manners that are dictated by intellect and a sense of right and wrong. This is called ethics. But we Jews are a holy people. Even regarding those commandments that deal with human relations and make human sense, we perform them only because God commanded us to do so in His holy Torah.[2]

⋘

How Does One Merit to Be a Jew?

A number of times, we heard Rabbi Nachman say with great longing, "How does one merit to be a Jew?" He said this sincerely and with great simplicity, as though he had not even yet begun.[3]

---

2. Source: *Sichot Haran*, no. 116.

3. Source: *Shivchei Haran*, *Sichot Haran* (Benei Brak, 5736), no. 33.

11

Torah

The Map of Time and Space

There was a king who had an object shaped like a hand, with five fingers and lines, just like a real hand.

This hand was the map of all the worlds. Everything that existed since heaven and earth were created until the very end and even afterward was illustrated on that hand. The lines and wrinkles of the hand illustrated in detail the structure of all the worlds, together with all the objects in each world. All of this was illustrated on the hand and in the lines and wrinkles of the hand, just like a map.

The lines of the hand formed letters. Just as letters are written on a map next to every object to identify it – a city, a river, and so on – the lines of the hand were like letters. The letters stood next to every object that was illustrated on the hand and identified it.

Each state, each city, all the rivers, bridges, mountains, and other things were illustrated in the lines and wrinkles of the hand. And next to each object stood letters telling what it is. All the people who lived in each state and everything that they lived

43

through was illustrated on the hand. Even all the roads from one state to the other and from one area to another were there. . . .

The pathway from one world to another world was illustrated there. There is a pathway on which one can go on from earth to heaven (people cannot go from earth to heaven because they do not know the way, but there the pathway by which one can go up to heaven was illustrated). All the pathways that exist between one world and the next were illustrated there.

Elijah went up to heaven on one pathway, and that pathway was illustrated there.

Moses went up to heaven on another pathway, and that pathway was illustrated there.

Enoch went up to heaven on another pathway, and that pathway was also illustrated there.

And so from one world to the next world, everything was illustrated in the lines and wrinkles of the hand.

Everything was illustrated as it had existed at the time that the world was created, as it is today, and as it will be in the future. For instance, there was an illustration of Sodom as it had been before it was overturned, there was an illustration of Sodom being overthrown, and there was another illustration of how Sodom looks today after having been overthrown.

Everything was illustrated on the hand: what was, what is, and what will be.[1]

€€€

Discipline and Liberation

Rabbi Nachman said, "I have very much wanted to inspire people to take on a discipline of learning a certain amount of Torah every day.

"Even people who are very far from holiness and who have become habitual sinners can be inspired by the great power of Torah to abandon their conduct. If they will only take on a strict

---

1. Source: *Sippurei Maasiyot,* "The Master of Prayer," p. 155.

schedule of a certain amount of learning per day, they will free themselves, for the power of Torah is immense."[2]

€€€

When the Torah Shows Its Love

Rabbi Nachman rebuked someone for not learning regularly. "Why don't you learn? What will you lose? To the contrary, you will receive the world-to-come. More than that, when the Torah shows its love to a person, he won't even want the world-to-come. He will only want the Torah itself. God Himself learns Torah. As our sages say, 'For the first three hours of the day, God learns Torah' (*Avodah Zarah* 3b).

"In these generations, due to our sins, Torah learning has become very lax.

"The great rabbis of previous generations didn't know about mystical intentions. Nevertheless, they could cause miracles with their Torah learning. Because of their Torah learning, when they simply said something, it came about."[3]

€€€

Dragging Evil to the Study Hall

"If this lowlife, the evil inclination, meets you, drag him to the study hall" (*Kiddushin* 30b).

At times, the evil inclination prays within a person. The person is like a synagogue in which someone is praying.

At other times, a person is like a study hall in which the evil inclination is learning.

The superior situation is that of the study hall. Our sages said that "if [the evil inclination] is a stone, it will melt [as a

---

2. Source: *Sichot Haran*, no. 19.
3. Source: *Sichot Haran*, no. 17.

result of one's learning]; if it is metal, it will explode"
(*Kiddushin* 30b).[4]

This is why our sages began by saying, "If this lowlife *meets*
you." The word used here for *meeting* refers homiletically to
prayer, as our sages pointed out (*Berachot* 26b). In other words,
when this lowlife is praying within you, and you are only like a
synagogue, drag him to the study hall, for it is better that one
become like a study hall, since that is more efficacious in dealing
with one's evil inclination.[5]

⋘

The Traveler through Torah

While still in this world, a person should go through all the Torah
literature, visiting every area of Torah.

The great princes tour various countries and spend vast sums
of money so that they will be able to boast afterward about all
the places that they visited.

In the same way, a person should visit all the different areas of
the Torah, so that when he arrives at the world-to-come, he will
be able to boast that he was in every place – that is, in every
book. Then he will be given the ability to recall everything he
had learned while in this world.[6]

⋘

Success through Visualization

If a person's thoughts regarding learning Torah are very strong,
then what he visualizes will come to pass. His thought must be

---

4. One's Torah learning will vitiate the force of the evil inclination.
The sages recommend that one treat the evil inclination by studying,
but they do not mention the option of praying.

5. Source: *Sichot Haran*, no. 104.

6. Source: *Sichot Haran*, no. 28.

very strong and determined. For instance, a person may visualize that he will learn the entire *Shulchan Aruch* (major source of Jewish law and custom) with its major commentaries. He visualizes how he will learn and in how much time – for instance, he will learn five pages a day and finish within a year. He has to visualize this very strongly until his imagination is bound up in it. The same goes for other areas of Torah learning, such as Talmud with the *Rif*, the *Rosh* and the *Turim, Tanakh*, and so on. He should desire this strongly and think about it deeply. As a result, he will successfully carry out his intentions.

Rabbi Nachman said that this is the meaning of the words of our sages (*Sanhedrin* 26b) that "a thought affects one's Torah learning." Even though Rashi understands this statement differently, this is what our sages mean. "Both opinions are the words of the living God" (*Gittin* 6b).[7]

⋘

Learning without Comprehension

A person should learn even if he doesn't understand.[8]

⋘

Understanding in the World-to-Come

Whatever one learned in this world and didn't completely understand, one will understand in the world-to-come.[9]

⋘

Forgetting and Recalling

We have learned (*Kohelet Rabbah* 1:34) that forgetfulness was created in order to make the Torah as continuously beloved as

---

7. Source: *Sichot Haran*, no. 62.

8. Source: *Sefer Hamidot* (Jerusalem: Zvi Latzaddik, 5745), Learning, no. 38.

9. Source: *Sefer Hamidot*, Learning, no. 8.

though one is just beginning. When a person relearns something
that he had forgotten, it is as though he is learning it for the first
time, and so he enjoys it. The rabbis told the following parable:
"A number of men were hired to fill up barrels. These barrels
were punctured, and everything that was poured into them
spilled out. The fools said, 'Since the liquid keeps spilling out,
why bother filling up the barrels?' But the wise man said, 'What
concern is it of mine? I get paid by the day, so what do I care if
it gets spilled?' Similarly, even if a person forgets what he has
learned, God will not deny him his daily payment" (*Vayikra
Rabbah* 19:2).

The *Zohar* teaches (Genesis 185a) that in the future, a person
will recall all of his learning that he had forgotten. Also, if a
person heard Torah from a true *tzaddik* and didn't understand
it, in the world-to-come he will understand. This is because
Torah is primarily geared to the soul. In the world-to-come, a
person's soul will be expert in Torah and will have a deep
understanding of what he had learned in this world. Fortunate is
the person who spends his time learning Torah and serving
God.[10]

€€€

Learning Aloud

When one learns Torah, one should speak the concepts aloud in
one's own language. This is good for the world.[11]

€€€

How to Learn Torah

I heard that Rabbi Nachman once mentioned that he had learned
all four sections of the *Shulchan Aruch* three times. The first

---

10. Source: *Sichot Haran*, no. 26.
11. Source: Likkutei Moharan 1:118.

time he learned it simply. The second time, he learned it in depth. He knew the source of each law in the Talmud, Rashi, and *Tosafot*. The third time, he understood the mystic reason behind every law.

He accomplished this while a youngster, for he afterward reviewed the *Shulchan Aruch* a number of times more.

Rabbi Nachman learned an extraordinary amount throughout his life, even until the end when he suffered from tuberculosis. He was beset with community responsibilities, working intensively with his disciples to bring us close to God and to show us how to serve God. In addition, his mind was always soaring among high and awesome realizations.

Nevertheless, every day he learned a great deal of Torah simply. He was never pressured, but always calm. He was quite extraordinary in this, in a way that is impossible to describe. That is why he had time to do everything.

He always learned exceptionally quickly. He would learn a few pages of *Shulchan Aruch* in one hour, together with all the commentaries on the page of the large edition: the *Turei Zahav*, the *Magen Avraham*, the *B'er Hagolah*, the *Pri Chadash*, the *Ateret Zekeinim*, and so on.

He said that when everyone else is getting ready to go to prayers in the morning, he learns four pages of *Shulchan Aruch*.

He learned everything – Talmud, *Shulchan Aruch* and so on – very quickly.

He spoke to us at length about this, saying that it is good to learn quickly without being pedantic. One should learn simply and fast. One shouldn't confuse oneself by comparing what one is learning in one place with what one recalls from another place. One should simply see that one understands the topic that one is presently learning.

At times, a person may not understand something. But he shouldn't spend too much time worrying about it. He should let it go and continue learning further. Usually, as a result of his steady learning, he will later come to understand what was puzzling him.

Rabbi Nachman said that in learning, one needs to do no more than simply say the words.

Then, in the process itself, one will come to understand.

One shouldn't confuse oneself when one first starts learning by trying to understand immediately. With such an attitude, a person will immediately run into problems, and he won't understand anything. Instead, he should put himself in the mind-set of learning. He should say the words quickly. Then he will eventually come to understand. If he doesn't understand now, he will understand later.

If there remain a number of matters that he still doesn't understand, what of it? He will have more than made up for that imperfection with the vast amount of learning that he has accomplished, for that is of supreme value. As our sages said, "A person should first learn and only then seek to understand, even if he doesn't know what he is saying" (*Shabbat* 63a).

As a result of his speed, he will learn a great deal and he will come to review the texts several times. As a result, he will understand the second or third time whatever he didn't grasp at first.

Rabbi Nachman spoke of this a great deal. It is impossible to clarify these matters fully in writing.

This is a truly wonderful approach to learning. Using this technique, one can learn an extraordinary amount, reading a vast amount of material and ultimately coming to understand them much better than if one had learned pedantically, for a stress on understanding every detail confuses a person very much. Many people stopped learning Torah entirely because they had been so concerned with details. In the end, they were left with nothing.

But when a person accustoms himself to learn quickly and without being overprecise, he will acquire the Torah. He will be able to learn a great deal: Talmud, *halachah*, *Tanach*, *Midrash*, *Zohar* and other books of Kabbalah, and all the other literature.

Rabbi Nachman said that every year, a person should learn the entire Talmud together with the commentaries of the *Rif* and the *Rosh*; the four sections of the *Shulchan Aruch* with its commentaries; all the collections of *midrash*; the *Zohar*, the *Tikkunei Zohar*, and the *Zohar Chadash*; and all the kabbalistic teachings of the *Ari*. In addition, a part of one's daily learning should be given over to learning with some degree of in-depth study.

Then he added a number of other things: a person should say psalms every day, as well a very great amount of prayers.

In the course of this talk, Rabbi Nachman began to discuss the idea that a person should learn very quickly without worrying about learning in-depth and comparing texts.

These techniques have been tested and found to work.[12]

Rabbi Nachman added that no one should be upset by his saying that a person should learn so much every day. Even if one doesn't manage to learn so much, one can still be a truly kosher person.

Previously, Rabbi Nachman had said that one can be a kosher person even if one doesn't know how to learn at all. One can even be a *tzaddik*, although one is not a scholar.

However, if one is not a scholar who is well versed in Talmud, with Rashi and *Tosafot*, one cannot master certain concepts. Still, even if a person is completely simple, he can become a kosher person and a complete *tzaddik*.

As our sages have said, "You are not required to complete the work, but neither are you free from engaging in it" (*Avot* 2:16).[13]

---

12. As Aryeh Kaplan has pointed out in *Rabbi Nachman's Wisdom*, Rabbi Nachman's schedule here is immense: 30,000 pages of material per year. It would be a full-time task for most people just to rush through and say the words, much less to have the most basic idea of what one is saying.

Nevertheless, there are many Torah leaders who have demonstrated remarkable abilities to learn Torah extraordinarily quickly and with great comprehension. For instance, Rav Kook learned fifty to sixty folios of Talmud per hour. Rabbi Nachman is giving a person a vote of confidence and expanding his horizons. This is similar to the breaking of the four-minute mile. Originally, such a feat was considered impossible. But as soon as it was broken, many other runners followed suit. Their own mental constraints had been expanded, and they now allowed themselves to accomplish what they had previously told themselves could not be done.

13. Rabbi Nachman's teachings can open the floodgates of Torah learning.

Rabbi Nachman did not say that a person should review his learning immediately. Rather, he should learn an entire book through from beginning to end quickly, and then learn it again in its entirety.[14]

❧❧❧

Creating One's Own Torah Thoughts

Rabbi Nosson heard that Rabbi Nachman had urged someone to learn his teachings and then to create his own novel Torah thoughts. Rabbi Nachman told that man, "If you understand exactly what I meant, that is excellent. But even if not, it is very good that you have created novel Torah thoughts.

"Creating novel Torah thoughts is a great rectification for thoughts of sin. All such thoughts are a result of the power of imagination. By using one's imagination to delve into the holy realm of Torah, one rectifies having previously misused it."

Rabbi Nachman said that creating original Torah thoughts is a great rectification for one's past. Even if one can only create one original word, that is good. This is also good for one's departed parents.[15]

One may never have felt the internal permission to simply learn without total understanding. Rabbi Nachman gives one conceptual permission to do so, and this may provide an intensely vibrant opportunity. Just saying the words of Torah can also be immensely slaking to a person's soul.

But at some point, a person's needs may change. Then, if he needs to learn in some other framework or to shift emphasis, he must go along with his organic, natural need.

Rabbi Nachman's statements may be best viewed as not ideal learning techniques presented in a vacuum, but as a balancing response to the imbalanced Torah learning that he saw about him.

Rabbi Nachman is a reservoir of opportunity, not a limited pool. And as Rabbi Nachman himself said, one should learn Torah from all masters.

14. Source: *Sichot Haran,* no. 76.
15. Source: *Likkutei Moharan* 2:105.

≪≪≪

God Enjoys One's Torah Thoughts

When a person creates novel Torah thoughts for the sake of heaven, he must believe in himself and believe that God derives a great deal of pleasure from his thoughts. He must not be lax. He must enthusiastically keep creating new insights and writing them down, until he produces books. As a result, all the strict judgments in the world will be ameliorated.[16]

≪≪≪

The *Tzaddikim* Have Paved the Way

Nowadays, it is very easy to create novel Torah thoughts. This is because a great deal of literature written by *tzaddikim* has been printed, and insights and concepts are in the air.[17]

≪≪≪

The Chambers of Torah Insight

There are chambers of Torah. If a person has reached their level, when he begins creating novel Torah thoughts, he enters these rooms. Then he passes from one room into the next. Each room has several doors that lead into other rooms. This person enters these rooms, and goes from one to the next.

These rooms are full of treasures. As the person creating the novel Torah thoughts passes through the rooms, he gathers these precious and lovely treasures.

However, one must be very careful not to fool oneself. One cannot reach such a level quickly.[18]

---

16. Source: *Likkutei Eitzot* (Jerusalem: Keren Hadpasa Dihasidei Breslov, 5736), Talmud Torah, no. 47.

17. Source: *Likkutei Moharan* 2:118.

18. Source: *Likkutei Moharan* 1:245.

〰〰〰

Creating Rivers of Torah

When one creates novel Torah thoughts, one creates rivers.

When one begins to create Torah thoughts, a spring begins to flow. This is referred to by the verse, "A spring will go out of the House of God" (Joel 4:18). The "House of God" is a person's mind. We see this from the verse, "In wisdom is a house built" (Proverbs 24:3).[19]

A spring is at first small and narrow. Afterward it grows deeper and broader, until rivers flow, and everyone comes to drink from those rivers.[20]

〰〰〰

Torah Insights Are on the Level of the Messiah

When a person creates new Torah insights, those insights are on the level of the messiah. This idea is referred to by the verse, "The spirit of God hovered over the face of the water" (Genesis 1:2). The *Zohar* explains that "the spirit of God" refers to the spirit of the messiah, and "the face of the water" refers to Torah (*Zohar Vayeishev* 192b).

When one creates insights into the Torah, that itself is the level of the messiah, for the messiah's spirit is right there with it.[21]

---

19.   That is to say, a house is connected to wisdom, which is one's mind.

20.   Similarly, when a person creates Torah thoughts, he creates a river of Torah and insight that can inspire and awaken others.

Source: *Likkutei Moharan* 1:262.

21.   When one creates new insights in Torah, one is actually connecting oneself to and drawing down into the world the liberating and redemptive power that, in its ultimate revelation, will come with

‹‹‹

Giving God Joy

When a person creates Torah insights, he gives God joy.[22]

‹‹‹

Speaking of Good

If you wish to bring any matter to life when you create a Torah insight, do not speak of evil matters but interpret verses that speak of good.[23]

‹‹‹

Cultivating Torah Insights

When a person is creating Torah thoughts, he should mentally repeat the verse or topic that he is studying over and over again, and he should pray until the door of understanding is opened for him.

Sometimes, a thought flashes through a person's mind. He has to have a great deal of strength to capture that thought.[24]

‹‹‹

The Protection of Learning Jewish Law

When a person creates novel Torah thoughts, he is surrounded by [hostile spiritual entities] that gaze on [and wish to make use of that energy].

the messianic age. Even in the midst of one's own exile, one can have access to and bring into oneself and the world actual pieces of that uncompromised power for redemptive change.

Source: *Likkutei Moharan* 1:118.
22. Source: *Sefer Hamidot*, Learning, no. 3.
23. Source: *Sefer Hamidot*, Learning, no. 2.
24. Source: *Sichot Haran*, no. 58.

Therefore, a person has to set up soldiers before and after himself, in order that no [hostile force] may approach him.

This is done by learning *halachah* – Jewish law. One must learn *halachah* both before and after creating novel Torah thoughts.

Then one is preceded and followed by soldiers. As a result, the Torah [that one learns] can descend [into the world that is permeated by evil influences] and one can walk safely among [those influences], for the armed soldiers do not allow them to approach [these Torah thoughts].[25]

€€€

Torah without Insights

Sometimes a person learns Torah, yet is unable to contribute any original insight of his own. This is because the intelligence of the Torah is as yet unborn.

This is the level of "Jacob." Jacob corresponds to pregnancy. This is referred to in the verse, "In the belly, he held the heel of his brother" (Hosea 12:4).[26]

Then, one has to cry out [to God in prayer]. This is referred to in the verse, "The voice is the voice of Jacob" (Genesis 27:22). When a person is on the level of Jacob, he has to cry out in many voices. As a result, he will bring forth the intelligence of the Torah so that it will be [actualized and] "born."

If a person learns Torah but has no original insights, he should not teach it to others. This Torah is [only] on the level of Jacob and pregnancy.

It is true that God delights in it. (This is referred to by a verse and our sages' comment on it. The verse reads, "His flag of love is above me" (Song of Songs 2:4). Our sages commented, "Do not read, 'his flag (*diglo*),' but rather 'his stammering (*ligligo*).' Even

---

25. Source: *Likkutei Moharan* 2:21.

26. The word for "held the heel of" is *akav*, related to the name "Jacob." So we see that Jacob is seen as corresponding to being "in the belly."

the stammering of a child is pleasing to God" (*Midrash Shir Hashirim* 2:13). However, one should not teach this in public as it is. One should only teach material that one has already clarified.

As our sages commented, "The verse says, 'Say to wisdom: you are my sister' (Proverbs 7:4). If the fact that something is forbidden by the Torah is as clear to you as your sister's identity, then you can give this Torah teaching in public. But if not, do not say it" (*Shabbat* 145b).

This idea is referred to in the verse, "God has chosen Jacob" (Psalms 135:4). When one's learning is in the category of Jacob and of pregnancy without [intrinsic] intelligence, God has chosen it for Himself—it is His 'stammering.'"

But the verse continues, "and Israel as His special one." When the letters of Israel are rearranged, they spell out, "My head." This refers to the revelation of the intelligence [of Torah] and the drawing down of the light of the [divine] "face," the divine efflux, into [one's] inner being. This [state of internalizing and understanding Torah] is referred to as Israel, as in the verse, "Israel, in you I will take pride" (Isaiah 49:3). "*In* you"—the beautiful crown of transcendental spiritual forces will be drawn *into* the [Jews'] inner being. Then Israel is called God's "special one." The Hebrew word for "special"—*segulah*—implies something that transcends nature.[27]

At that point, one is ready to teach the Torah to others.[28]

❦❦❦

Clarifying One's Character through *Halachah*

Rabbi Nachman particularly urged us to learn *halachah*—Jewish law. A person should learn all four sections of the *Shulchan*

---

27. When one draws Torah into one's inner being and clarifies it by subjecting it to the process of one's insight, then one draws the transcendent nature of the Torah into oneself.

28. Source: *Likkutei Moharan* 1:21:8.

Aruch from beginning to end. If he can learn with the major commentaries, that is best. But if not, he should at least learn the main text.

This is a very great rectification. When a person sins, he mixes together good and evil, [confusing what is forbidden with what is allowed]. By learning *halachah*, which clarifies what is kosher and what is unkosher, what is allowed and what is forbidden, what is pure and what is impure, he clarifies the good from the evil.

Rabbi Nachman said that every Jew is obligated to learn *halachah* every day. Even if he is rushed, he should learn at least one paragraph of any part of the Shulchan Aruch. When he isn't rushed, he should learn the four sections of the *Shulchan Aruch* day by day. After he finishes all four sections of the *Shulchan Aruch*, he should go through them again. He should conduct himself this way for all of his life.[29]

⁝

Separating Good from Evil

Through Torah and prayer, one attains the ability to separate evil from good and to nullify evil.

In learning, one should "come to rest in the depths of *halachah*" (see *Megillah* 3b)—that is, one should learn *halachah*. The Torah is grasped by both good and evil forces. They gain access to the Torah through its laws of prohibition and permission, impurity and purity, kosher and not kosher.

Until a person clarifies the *halachah*, good and evil remain mixed. As a result, he cannot separate the evil from the good and nullify the evil. He remains on the level referred to by the verse, "If a person seeks evil, it will come to him" (Proverbs 11:27).

But when a person studies and clarifies the *halachah*, determining what is allowed and what is forbidden, and so on, he

---

29. Today there are many English-language books of *halachah* dealing with all areas of life.

Source: *Sichot Haran*, no. 29.

becomes capable of separating good from evil (see *Zohar Bahar* 111b).[30]

≪≪≪

The Gates of Eden

There are two levels to the Garden of Eden: the garden, and Eden. These refer to the levels of higher wisdom and lower wisdom.

The pleasure of the Garden of Eden consists primarily in the attainment of divine wisdom, which comprises both higher and lower wisdom.

One can attain this only via the gates that surround the Garden of Eden, through which one enters and attains both higher and lower wisdom.

These gates are hidden and sunken within the ground. As the verse says, "Its gates are sunken in the ground" (Lamentations 2:9).

One needs a person to rule the earth. This person can draw out and set up these gates that have sunken into the earth.

By learning *halachah*, one can become such a ruler. Then one can set up the gates that had sunken into the earth. This is referred to by the verse, "The king will set up the earth with judgment" (Proverbs 29:4). "Judgment" refers to *halachah*. That is, through the laws of the Torah—i.e., by learning *halachah* and clarifying what the Torah law is—one becomes a ruler and king. Then one can set up the earth and one can reveal the gates that had sunken into the earth.

As a result, one attains the Garden of Eden.[31]

≪≪≪

Learning *Zohar*

It is well known that learning *Zohar* is a powerful spiritual technique.

---

30. Source: *Likkutei Moharan* 1:86.
31. Source: *Likkutei Moharan* 1:286.

When one learns *Zohar,* one creates a powerful desire to learn all aspects of the holy Torah.

The holy language of the *Zohar* is very influential in awakening a person to serve God. When the *Zohar* refers to a person who serves God, it uses the phrase "*Zaka'a*" – "Happy is he." And to the contrary, the *Zohar* cries out, "*Vai ley, vai lenishmatei*" – "Woe, woe to the soul of that person," regarding anyone who turns aside from serving God.

These phrases have a very powerful effect on influencing a person to serve God.[32]

***

Learning Unhappy Matters

When one learns unhappy matters, such as the laws of mourning, one should not study them much. One should not invest one's thoughts in such areas. Since thought has such great power, one should pass over these areas quickly.[33]

***

Yearning to Learn

It may be that a person finds it impossible to learn – whether he does not know how to learn, or he doesn't have a book with him, and so on. Nevertheless, his heart burns within him and longs greatly to learn Torah and serve God. This very desire to learn is on the level of learning from a book of Torah.

Sometimes, there are two *tzaddikim* in the world who are talking with one another. But they are hundreds of miles apart.

One *tzaddik* asks a question on the Torah, and the other *tzaddik* says something that answers the question of the first *tzaddik.*

---

32. Source: *Sichot Haran,* no. 108.
33. Source: *Sichot Haran,* no. 8.

Sometimes both *tzaddikim* ask a question, and the question of one answers the question of the other.

In this way, these two *tzaddikim* talk with one another. But only God hears them.

This is referred to in the verse, "Those who fear God were speaking, one to the other" (Malachi 3:16). The Hebrew word for "were speaking" is written in a passive form, to indicate that they aren't literally speaking with each other, but that their communication occurs of itself, when one asks a question and another offers the answer.

Only God hears this conversation. This is referred to by the next words in the verse, "God gave heed and listened." Only God hears them and binds their words together.

Then God writes their words in a book. This is referred to by the next words in the verse, "He wrote a book of remembrance."

This book, in which the words of the *tzaddikim* are written, is on the level of the spiritual, supernal heart upon which the words of the *tzaddikim* are written. This is referred to in the verse, "Write them [the words of Torah] on the tablet of your heart" (Proverbs 3:3).

When this person's heart burns within him with the desire to learn Torah—but it is impossible for him to do so—he receives a heart from the supernal heart, which is on the level of the book of remembrance. It was from there that his initial desire to learn originated.

Then he is considered as though he has actually learned from a book. As the verse in Malachi continues, "He wrote a book of remembrance before Him for those who fear God and regard His name" (Malachi 3:16). Our sages remarked on this verse, "If a person only considers doing a *mitzvah* but is unable to do so, he is considered as though he actually did it" (*Berachot* 6a).

The very fact that the person's heart yearns and desires is considered an accomplished act.

This is because his desire to learn came from the supernal heart, which is the book of remembrance.

This idea can be seen as being referred to in the verse, "He wrote a book of remembrance before Him for those who fear God and regard His name." The "book of remembrance" is made

by the dialogue of the two *tzaddikim*. This book is for the sake
of "those who fear God and regard His name"—the person who
desires to learn Torah but who, for whatever reason, finds it
impossible to do so. As a result of his strong desire, this person
receives something from this book, which is also the supernal
heart.

In line with this thought, we can look at the situation of
Abraham. Abraham is called "the first convert" [to Judaism]
(*Sukkah* 49b). He had no one else from whom to learn. All he
had was the heart. He yearned so strongly to serve God that he
received from the supernal heart, which is also called a book of
remembrance.

At that time, there were no other *tzaddikim* in the world. So
what could be written on this supernal heart and book of
remembrance? [The answer is that] the supernal heart had
written on it the Torah insights of the *tzaddikim* who preceded
creation [spiritual entities, including the souls of *tzaddikim*,
preceded the creation of this physical world].

This is why Abraham is called a "rock." The verse says, "Look
to the rock from which you were hewn" (Isaiah 51:1), and our
sages say that this refers to Abraham (Rashi, there).

[Since Abraham is symbolized by the word "rock," we can
look at the verse,] "rock of my heart" (Psalms 73:6) and infer
that Abraham, the "rock," had nothing besides a "heart" that
burned to serve God.

This explains why all converts to Judaism are called by his
name, as in the verse, "The nobles of the nations gathered [in
Jerusalem to follow] the nation of the God of Abraham" (Psalms
47:10).[34]

Furthermore, why are converts called "nobles"? This word in
Hebrew means "giving" and is thus connected to the verse, "A
giving heart" (Exodus 35:5). Converts to Judaism are those who
have hearts that [are giving to God and] burning for God, just as
Abraham did.[35]

---

34. That is to say, the noble converts follow God, referred to
specifically as the God of Abraham, thus linking converts and Abraham.

35. Source: *Likkutei Moharan* 1:142.

Sleep and the Talmud

There are different types of sleep.

There is physical sleep, which affords rest to the mind.

Then there is learning the simple meaning of the Torah, which is called sleep when compared to cleaving to God (*Zohar Pinchas* 244b; see *Bereshit Rabbah Vayeitzei*, chap. 69). [The "simple meaning of Torah" means exoteric learning, as opposed to kabbalistic studies.]

Our sages commented on the verse, "You have placed me in the dark places" (Lamentations 3:6), that "[dark places] refers to the Babylonian Talmud, [whose logic can be confusing]" (*Sanhedrin* 24).[36]

Sleep is on the level of faith. As the verse says, "Your faithfulness is at night, [the time of sleep]" (Psalms 92:3). [To prove that night is equivalent to "darkness," we have the verse,] "[God] called the darkness night" (Genesis 1:5).

If a person is constantly clinging to the service of God and his mind grows weary due to his high level of cleaving, he should learn the simple meaning of the Torah. When he learns this simple meaning, his mind – that is, his soul – will enter the realm of faith.

This is referred to in the verse, "Every new morning, Your faithfulness is great" (Lamentations 3:23).[37]

Then, one's mind is renewed and invigorated from its weariness.[38]

◄◄◄

Dozing Off While Learning

Even learning Torah while one is dozing off is good.[39]

---

36. Darkness, which is related to sleep, has to do with Talmud learning, as opposed to kabbalistic learning.

37. When entering faith, one is renewed, as with a new morning.

38. Source: *Likkutei Moharan* 35:4.

39. Source: *Sefer Hamidot*, Learning, no. 6.

❧❧❧

Who Sows But Does Not Reap

A person who learns but doesn't review is like a farmer who sows but doesn't reap.[40]

❧❧❧

New Torah Literature

Once, we were talking with Rabbi Nachman about the fact that nowadays a great many Torah books, both old and new, are being published.

Rabbi Nachman mentioned that our sages said, "In the future, the Jews will forget the Torah" (*Shabbat* 138b). Many books are being printed, and everyone buys books so that the Torah will not be forgotten. Nowadays, even a tailor has books. "But," Rabbi Nachman continued, "people don't understand that if they don't learn Torah, having all these books doesn't help. And for our sins, Torah learning has become very weak and infrequent."[41]

---

40. Source: *Sefer Hamidot*, Learning, no. 50.
41. Source: *Sichot Haran*, no. 18.

12

Song

Even if You Cannot Sing Well, Sing

Rabbi Nachman said that a person should regularly cheer himself by singing. A tune is a very great thing, with the power to awaken a person and draw his heart to God.

Even if a person cannot sing well, he can at least sing when he is alone.

One cannot imagine the worth of a tune.[1]

❮❮❮

Holy Music Cleans the World

Music of holiness is on an extraordinarily high level, as is well known. The essence of such music is created when good is clarified and removed from evil. When one removes and separates good points from evil, music is formed.

When a person doesn't allow himself to fall, but rejuvenates

---

1. Source: *Sichot Haran*, no. 273.

himself by searching within himself and finding good points, and he gathers these good points out of the bad that is also within him, tunes are formed.

Then this person is able to pray, sing to God, and praise Him.

When a person grows disappointed with himself, with his corporeality and his wrong acts, and he sees that he is very far from true spirituality, he usually cannot pray at all. Because of his depression, bitterness, and heaviness, he cannot open his mouth, seeing how far he is from God.

But despite his knowledge of his many wrong acts and his great distance from God, a person must revivify himself. He must search within himself and find his good points. He must revivify himself and rejoice with this, for a person should rejoice with every good point that he can find within himself. Then he can pray, sing, and praise God. As the verse says, "I will sing to my God with my being" (Psalms 146:2).

Know that the person who can make such tunes by gathering these good points from every Jew, even from Jewish sinners, is able to lead the communal prayers.

The prayer leader is called the *shaliach tzibbur*—the representative of the congregation. He must be sent by all the congregation. He must gather all the good points that are found in every one of the congregation. All these good points must be incorporated within him.

Then he stands and prays with all this goodness. This is the role of the "representative of the congregation."

He must be on such a high level that all the good points desire to come to him and are incorporated within him.

A person who can make such tunes—i.e., who can judge every individual favorably, even frivolous or bad people, by searching out their good points—such a person is a *tzaddik* who can represent the congregation.[2]

€€€

---

2. Source: *Likkutei Moharan* 1:282.

❦❦❦

Instrumental Music Clarifies the Imagination

One subjugates the power of fantasy via the level referred to as a "hand." This is referred to in the verse, "I will be imagined via the hand of the prophets" (Hosea 12:11).

The concept of "hand" is in turn related to that of joy. As the verse says, "You will rejoice in everything to which you send your hand" (Deuteronomy 12:7).

This is related to musical instruments that one plays with one's hand, via which the spirit of prophecy rests on the prophets. As Elisha the prophet commanded, "Bring me a musician" (2 Kings 3:16).

An instrument has gathered in it various spirits that are a mixture of good and evil. There is a depressed spirit (as in Proverbs 15:13), an evil spirit. As is said of Saul, "An evil spirit frightened him" (1 Samuel 16:14).

On the other hand, there is a good spirit, as in the verse, "[With] Your good spirit, lead me in a smooth land" (Psalms 143:10). This is the spirit of prophecy and holiness.

When the good and evil spirits are mixed together, one cannot receive a true prophecy.

We learn that Saul "prophesied . . . and he fell, naked" (1 Samuel 19:34). Rashi explains, "He acted madly." [Saul acted in this way] because a foolish and depressed spirit was mixed in him.

When a person plays a musical instrument with his hands, he gathers the good spirit, the spirit of prophecy, from the depressed spirit. Such a person must be one who "knows how to play music" (1 Samuel 16:18), who knows how to gather the correct notes and thus create the tune, which is related to joy.

One must be able to build a good spirit, a spirit of prophecy, which is the opposite of a depressed spirit.

One must be able to play one's instrument, going up and down with one's hand, and intending to build perfect joy.

When the prophet hears such a tune from one who knows how to play, he receives his spirit of prophecy from [the tune] that was gathered by the musician's hand from the depressed spirit.[3]

This is referred to by the verse, "He will play with his hand, and it will be good for you" (1 Samuel 16:16). "It will be good for you"—for he is gathering the "good" from the bad. This process of gathering and building the spirit of prophecy is accomplished with the hand. Via the concept of the hand, souls come to God to be judged by Him. As the verse says, "In Your hand, I will place my soul" (Psalms 31:6).

This is related to the subjugation of fantasy, which is on the level of an evil spirit, a spirit of foolishness that desires to confuse the good spirit, the spirit of prophecy. This fantasy is subjugated by the joy that comes about through the music played by the musician's hand.

Fantasy is strengthened by depression, since fantasy is on the level of a depressed spirit, an evil spirit, which confuses the good spirit, the spirit of prophecy.

One can only receive a spirit of prophecy and holiness via joy, which is the level of playing a musical instrument.

This is related to the verse, "I will recall my tune at night; I will speak with my heart, and my spirit shall search" (Psalms 77:7).

The night is the time that souls rise up to God to be judged by Him. That is the time to gather the good spirit from the evil spirit. That is the most propitious time to engage in *hitbodedut*, i.e., to pray to God in one's own words, to speak out one's heart and to seek the good spirit—i.e., the good points that one still possesses—to clarify them from the evil spirit.[4]

This is the level of the tune, through which one's memory is guarded—i.e., one's ability to keep one's mind on one's ultimate purpose, the world-to-come, and to cleave mentally to the supernal world.[5]

---

3. Rabbi Nachman weaves together literal and symbolic meaning so smoothly that it is hard to tell where one begins and the other leaves off.

4. Apparently, the musical instrument symbolizes the practice of *hitbodedut*.

5. Source: *Likkutei Moharan* 1:54:6.

€€€

The Melody of Faith

Via his tune, the *tzaddik* raises souls from heresy.

Every wisdom has its own tune from which it is derived.

Even heresy has its special tune.

The higher a wisdom is, the higher is its corresponding tune. Ultimately, one rises to the very beginning of creation, the beginning of emanation. There is nothing higher than that level. It is surrounded by nothing but the light of the infinite God, within which is contained all creation and wisdoms.

That level also has a level of wisdom, but this level of wisdom cannot be apprehended, for the Infinite One is God Himself, and it is impossible to understand His wisdom. Only faith applies there – belief that the Infinite One's light surrounds all the universes.

Faith has its own special tune. As we can see, even each idolatrous faith has its own tunes that it sings in its house of worship.

The opposite holds true for holiness. Each faith has its own tune.

As for the faith that is higher than all wisdoms and other faiths – i.e., the faith in the light of the Infinite One Himself that surrounds all the world – its tune is correspondingly higher than all the tunes in the world that correspond to each wisdom and faith.

All the tunes of all the faiths are themselves drawn from this one tune that is higher than all the tunes of all the wisdoms. This is because this tune relates to the faith in the light of the Infinite One Himself, Who is higher than everything.

In the future, "The nations will have a clear speech to call together in the name of God" (Zephaniah 3:9). Then everyone will believe in God.

Then the verse, "Come, gaze from the head of Amanah" (Song of Songs 4:8) will be fulfilled. The name Amanah is related to *emunah* – faith. The "head of Amanah" refers to this highest faith.

The word for "gaze"—*tashuri*—is related to the word for tune—*shir*. Thus, we can read the verse, "Come and sing the tune of the highest level of faith."

[As for now, however], only the *tzaddik* of the generation is able to attain this tune of supernal faith. Therefore, via the tune of the *tzaddik*, all the souls who fell into the heresy of the "empty vacuum" rise and emerge. This is because the *tzaddik*'s tune is on the level of the supernal faith. Via this faith and its tune, all heresy is nullified. Then, all tunes are gathered and nullified within this tune, which is higher than everything, and from which are drawn all the wisdoms.[6]

≪≪≪

The New Song of the Future

In the future, when the world is renewed, the entire universe will operate on the level of wonders, according to providence alone, and not according to nature.

Then a new song shall arise. As the verse says, "Sing a new song to God, for He has done wonders" (Psalms 98:1).

---

6. No intellectual, verbal wisdom is complete in itself. Rather, it is the finite expression of a spiritual state that transcends borders and words. This spiritual state exists on an objective, spiritual level and can be accessed by a human being's soul and felt within him as a subjective feeling. The highest such wordless state of consciousness is higher than all wisdoms and intellect. This state is total openness to the awareness of God's existence. When one has such a consciousness, a consciousness that transcends the boundaries of intellect and human limitation, one perceives God and Godliness in an ideal and ultimate manner. One is immediately aware that everything—all wisdoms and all other states of transcendent consciousness—are mere branches of the Godliness that permeates all creation. Everything else is nullified by and swallowed up into this light of infinite being.

Melody puts one in touch with this wordless, higher state of consciousness. A holy melody, like this state of consciousness, has both an objective spiritual status and a subjective, affective influence on a person.

Source: *Likkutei Moharan* 1:64:5.

This song of the future is a song of God's providence, a song of wonders.

There is also a song of nature, as in the verse, "The heavens tell the glory of God, the work of His hands are proclaimed by the firmament" (Psalms 19:2). This is the song of nature, of the astronomical laws. This is the level of song and praise that is sung to God for the way the world is run now, via nature.

But in the future, there will be a new song, a song of wonders, of providence, for then the world will be ruled by providence alone.[7]

---

7. Source: *Likkutei Moharan* 2:8:10.

13

Stories

Folk Tales and Holy Secrets

Before telling the first story in this book, Rabbi Nachman said, "In the stories that the world tells, there are many secrets and very high matters. But the stories have been corrupted. There is a great deal that is missing, and they are confused and not told in the proper order. That which belongs to the beginning is told at the end, and the like.

"But those stories really contain very hidden and high matters.

"The Baal Shem Tov was able to make Unifications through a story. When he saw that the supernal channels were corrupted and it was impossible to rectify them with prayer, he would rectify and unify them with a story."

Most of the stories that Rabbi Nachman told are completely original. They came from his heart and holy knowledge, inspired by the high level that he attained with his holy spirit, which he would clothe within the story. The story itself is an awesome vision that he attained and saw on his level.

At other times, he would retell a popular story. But he would add a great deal and change around its order, until it was very different.

When Rabbi Nachman began telling stories, he said clearly, "I will start telling stories." His meaning was that since he hadn't succeeded in bringing people close to God with his lessons, he would do so with his stories.[1]

❮❮❮

Stories Wake People Up

People say that stories are good for putting one to sleep. But I say that through stories, people can be woken from their sleep.[2]

---

1. Source: *Sippurei Massiyot*, introduction.
2. Source: *Chayei Moharan* 1:16, no. 25.

14

Humor

Foolish Things

A person has to constantly make himelf happy. In most circumstances, a person has to cheer himself up with foolish things,
with humor and jokes, in order to make himself as happy as
possible. Depression is the most harmful of negative traits and
the most difficult to overcome. As a result, in most cases, one
can only bring oneself to joy in this way.[1]

❮❮❮

The Story of the Humble King

Once upon a time, there was a king who had a wise advisor. The
king told his advisor, "There is another king who claims on his
seal that he is very powerful and also a truthful and humble man.

"As for his being powerful, I know that is true. His country is

---

1. Source: *Chayei Moharan* 2:72, no. 141.

surrounded by the sea. His navy stands on the sea with cannon
and doesn't let anyone pass through. Within the sea, large
swamps surround the country. Only one small path passes
through them, on which only one man can travel. There are also
cannon set up there. When someone comes to attack the
country, the cannon shoot at him and prevent anyone from
entering.

"But as for his claim that he is a truthful and humble man, I do
not know about that.

"So I want you to bring me that king's portrait."

This king had the portraits of all the kings with that one
exception, because no king had the portrait of that king. That
king was hidden from people; he sat behind a curtain, far away
from the people of his country.

The wise man went to that county. He decided that he must
know the quality of the country, how the country operates. And
how can he know the quality of the country? Through its
humor.

When one wants to know something, one must know the jokes
that relate to it.

There are various types of jokes. Sometimes, a person wants
to harm someone else with his words, and when the other person
protests, he says, "I was only joking." As the verse says, "Like
one who shoots firebrands, arrows and deadly weapons, and
says, I am merely joking" (Proverbs 26:18–19).

Other times, someone only means to make a joke, but his
words hurt the other person.

There are all types of jokes.

There is a country that is the archetype of all other countries.
This country contains a city that is the archetype of all its cities.
This city contains a house that is the archetype of all the houses
in the city. In that house is a person who is the archetype of all
the houses. A person is there who makes all the humor and jokes
of the entire country.

The wise man took a great deal of money with him, and went
there.

He saw that the people there were engaged in various kinds of tricks and jokes. He understood that the jokes of that country were filled with falsehood. He saw that when people did business, they cheated each other. When a person filed a claim in court, the court was full of lies and the judges took bribes. When he went to the higher court, it too was full of lies. And they used to make humorous skits of all these things.

The wise man understood from these jokes that the country was full of lies and cheating, and that there was no truth there whatsoever.

He began to engage in business in the country, and let himself be cheated. He filed a claim in the courts. The judges were all full of lies and took bribes.

One day he would give a bribe, and the next day they would claim not to recognize him.

He went to a higher court, and that too was filled with lies. Finally, he came before the supreme court.

The supreme court was also filled with lies and bribery.

At last, he came to the king himself.

When he came to the king, he called out, "Over whom are you a king? From beginning to end, the country is filled with lies. There isn't any truth here whatsoever." He began to describe all of the falsehood of the country.

When the king heard these words, he bent his ear to the curtain. It was a great wonder to the king that someone should know the falseness of the county. When the ministers heard him, they grew very angry. But he continued to speak out and describe the falsehood of the country.

The wise man called out, "One might say that the king is like everyone else, that you also love falsehood. But the opposite is true. One can see that you are a man of truth. You are far from the people because you cannot stomach the lies of the country."

He began to praise the king extravagantly.

The king was very humble. "Where his greatness was, there was his humility" (*Megillah* 31a). This is the way of a humble person; the more he is praised, the more humble does he become in his own eyes.

Since the wise man praised the king so much, the king became extremely humble, until he became absolutely nothing.

He could not hold himself back, and he threw aside the curtain to see the wise man. "Who is this man who knows and understands all of this?"

The king's face was revealed. The wise man saw it. He painted his portrait and brought it to his king.[2]

---

2. Source: *Sippurei Maasiyot*, "The Humble King," p. 48.

15

The *Tzaddik*

How to Become a *Tzaddik*

Rabbi Nachman was upset with those people who held that a person can become a *tzaddik* only because he has a very high soul.

He said that this is not so. The matter depends on good deeds, hard work, and service of God.

He said explicitly that anyone can come to the highest level. Everything depends only on a person's will—he just has to have mercy on himself and clarify what is truly good for him.

Everything is in accordance with the extent of one's actions.[1]

<<<

Recognizing the *Tzaddik*

Some people mistakenly believe that one must recognize the *tzaddik* by his face and appearance, or that his appearance and movements will be unusual. But this is not so. The *tzaddik* has

---

1. Source: *Sichot Haran,* no. 26.

the same appearance as anybody else. Nevertheless, he is completely different from other people, and he really does not
resemble other people at all.

A holy Jew appears to go about with the same insides as any
other human being, but he is really a totally different being.[2]

⋘

Looking for the Best

The world says that a person doesn't have to look for great
things. But I say that one has to search only for great things.

One has to search for the greatest *tzaddik* and teacher.[3]

⋘

The Man of Compassion

1. "He who has compassion on them will lead them" (Isaiah
49:10).

A person who has compassion is fit to be a leader.

He must know how to handle his compassion. One may not be
compassionate to evil people, murderers, or thieves. Also, if a
person doesn't know how to handle his compassion, he may
decide to give a four-day-old baby food fit for someone older.
Such a baby must be fed only milk.

One must know how to handle one's compassion. When one is
compassionate to a baby, one gives him milk, and when one is
compassionate to an older person, one gives him food fit for him.
Similarly, one must be compassionate for everyone by giving
him what he needs.

2. Only Moses was this type of compassionate person. He was
the leader of Israel, and he will be the leader in the future. "That
which was will be" (Ecclesiastes 1:4).

---

2. Source: *Likkutei Moharan* 2:116.
3. Source: *Sichot Haran*, no. 51.

Moses had true compassion for Israel. He sacrificed himself for the sake of Israel and was ready to cast away his life without a moment's consideration for himself. God told him, "I will make you a great nation" (Exodus 32:10). But he did not pay any attention. Instead, he said, "Please forgive their sin" (Exodus 32).

He was a true, compassionate leader, and he worked for the good of the world so that the world would be civilized.

This is because the essence of a person is his understanding.

Whoever doesn't have understanding is not considered part of civilization, and is not even a human being. He is only an animal in human form.

Moses had compassion, and he worked for the sake of spreading civilization, so that the world should be populated by human beings, by people with understanding.

He opened the light of understanding for us, as in the verse, "You have seen to understand that the Lord is God" (Deuteronomy 4:35).

Moses opened up understanding and revealed that there is a God Who rules the earth.

3. The essential quality of compassion is to realize that when Israel (which is a holy nation) sins, that is the most pitiful thing.

The worst sufferings in the world are nothing compared to the heavy burden of sins.

When Israel sins, it has to carry an unbearably heavy burden. As the verse states, "Like a heavy burden, [my sins] are too heavy for me" (Psalms 38:5).

When a person realizes the holiness of Israel – the Jews' supernal source, their spirituality, and their extraordinary qualities – he knows that Israel is completely removed from sin, and that in the context of their extraordinary essential holiness, they have nothing to do with sin.

Therefore, all the sufferings in the world are considered as nothing in relation to the weight of sins.

Even if a person suffers, as long as those sufferings aren't a result of sinning, they are not even considered suffering. This is on the level of the statement, "There is no suffering without sin"

(*Shabbat* 55a) – if the experiences aren't a result of sin, they are not suffering. The essence of suffering is only related to sin. That is the most pitiable thing. One must have compassion on Israel, a holy nation, and draw them out from under the heavy weight of sin.

Whenever the Jews committed a sin, Moses would sacrifice himself for their sake and pray for them.

He knew that in relation to their holiness and extraordinary qualities, they are far removed from sin, and they cannot bear its heavy burden.

Where do sins come from? They are a result of a lack of understanding. "A man does not commit a sin unless a spirit of folly has entered into him" (*Sotah* 3a). This is the greatest pity of all. One must have compassion on a person who has sinned and fill him with understanding. The verse states, "Fortunate is the one who gives wisdom to the poor" (Psalms 41:2). Our sages said that "poverty refers to [lack of] understanding" (*Nedarim* 41a). One must have compassion on this person and fill him with understanding.[4]

≪≪≪

Mercy, the Heart, and the Spring

The true man of mercy is a very great man. I (that is, the stutterer who was telling this story) gather together all the true acts of mercy, and I bring them to the true man of mercy.

Time exists only as a result of true acts of mercy.

I gather together all the true acts of mercy and bring them to the true man of mercy.

From them, time is created.

There is a mountain. On the mountain is a stone. From the stone flows a spring.

And everything has a heart. The entire world has a heart. The heart of the world is a complete being, with a face and hands and

---

4. Source: *Likkutei Moharan* 2:7.

feet. The nail of the toe of the heart of the world has more heart than any other heart.

The mountain with the spring are at one end of the world. And the heart of the world is at the other end of the world.

The heart stands opposite the spring and constantly longs to come to it. The yearning of the heart for the spring is very deep. The heart constantly calls out that it wants to come to the spring.

And the spring also longs for the heart.

The heart has two weaknesses. One is due to the sun chasing it and burning it. The other weakness is because of its constant yearning and longing. It reaches out to the spring, and it calls out that it wishes to come to the spring. The heart stands opposite the spring and calls out.

It yearns more and more for the spring.

When the heart needs to rest and catch its breath, a great bird comes. It spreads its wings over the heart and shields it from the sun.

Then the heart rests a little.

But even while it is resting, it looks to the spring with yearning.

Since it yearns so much for the spring, why doesn't it go there?

As soon as the heart starts to move to the mountain where the spring is, it no longer sees the top of the mountain, so it can't see the spring. As soon as it doesn't see the spring, it starts to die, for the life force of the heart is drawn only from the spring.

If the heart were to die, the entire world would be destroyed, for the heart is the life force of everything. And how can the world exist without the heart?

So the heart cannot go to the spring. It stands constantly opposite the spring, longing and crying out constantly that it wishes to come to the spring.

As for the spring, it has no time at all. It is not within the realm of time.

If so, how can the spring be in the world?

The time of the spring comes only because the heart gives the spring a day as a present. When the day comes to an end, the spring will have no time, and it will leave the world.

If the spring no longer exists, the heart will die. Then the entire world will cease to exist.

When the end of the day comes close, the heart and spring begin to part from one another. They begin to tell each other very beautiful parables and poems with great love and longing for each other – the heart for the spring, and the spring for the heart.

The true man of mercy watches over this. When the day comes to its very end, just before it ends, the true man of mercy comes and gives the heart a day.

The heart gives the day to the spring.

Then the spring once again has time.

When the new day arrives, it brings with it parables and beautiful songs that contain all wisdoms.

Each day has a different quality. There is Sunday, Monday, and so on. There is also a first day of the month and the holidays.

All the time that the true man of mercy has comes through me, for I (the stutterer) am the one who goes out and gathers together all the true acts of mercy, from which time is created.[5]

⋐⋐⋐

The *Tzaddik* Is Both Above and Below

The *tzaddik*'s perfection is expressed in the fact that he is both above and below. He can show a person above who imagines that he is on a high level that the opposite is true. And he can show a person who is on the lowest level, in the very earth, that he is close to God.

If the *tzaddik* does not have this ability, he is not a *tzaddik*.

He must show the person who is on the lowest level that he is still close to God. He must awaken him and show him, "God is

---

5. Then the ability to grow and serve God within time is a gift of love. It is the *tzaddik*, the compassionate leader, who provides the gift of time. When time exists, the universe can exist, for the structure of polarity and tension can then exist.

Source: *Sippurei Maasiyot,* "The Seven Beggars," p. 210.

with you; do not be afraid, for He is next to you, because 'the entire earth is full of His glory' (Isaiah 6:3)."

Even if a person falls to the lowest rung, he can still cling to God and return to Him.

A person can encourage himself with the very fact that he realizes how far he is from God, because at first he didn't even know that. And now that he knows how far he is, that itself means that he is coming close to God.[6]

❮❮❮

The Light That Shines in a Thousand Universes

There is a light that shines in a thousand universes. This light is so great that a simple person cannot receive it. It needs a great, wise man who can divide thousands into hundreds. This person can divide the great light into smaller portions so that other people can receive it bit by bit. This is like a person who creates a very large insight into Torah. People aren't able to understand it, since it is impossible to understand half a teaching. But when he divides it into separate topics and sections, people can understand each part separately.

There is a light that shines in a thousand worlds and that is one understanding: it can only be understood as one unit but not in part, for it is one simple light.

A Torah scholar who is "vengeful" can divide the thousands into hundreds; he can divide the great light into divisions that people can receive.

This idea of the "vengeful scholar" who can divide the thousands into hundreds is explained in the verse, "He who goes over a matter [in bitter rumination] separates [himself from] the Master" (Proverbs 17:9). Rashi explains, "He is vengeful and rehearses over what his fellow did to him, and so he removes the Master of the world."

---

6. Source: *Likkutei Moharan* 2:68.

A scholar must be vengeful, as our sages said, "If a Torah scholar is not vengeful as a snake, he is not a Torah scholar" (*Yoma* 22b).

The verse can be explained in the following way: a Torah scholar who is vengeful can divide the thousands into hundreds. "And goes over the matter"—he is vengeful—then, "he separates the Master—*Aluf*—related to the word, *elef*: thousand"—he divides the thousands into hundreds.

This relates to the saying of our sages, "If you see a Torah scholar who is vengeful as a snake, gird him to your loins, for in the end you will benefit from his teaching" (*Shabbat* 63b). Because he is vengeful, he will be able to divide the thousands into hundreds, he will divide the great light into smaller sections. Then you will be able to benefit from his teaching and to receive from him, for it would otherwise be impossible to receive it, since it is such a great light.

The reason that only someone who is "vengeful" can achieve this is very, very deep.

The person who knows this can revive the dead. As our sages said, "In the future, *tzaddikim* will revive the dead" (*Pesachim* 68a; *Zohar Genesis* 114b, 135a). Such a person knows what death is. By dividing thousands into hundreds and drawing the thousands into the hundreds, death—*mavet*—is turned into hundreds—*meyot*—because the thousands have entered them.

If a person does not know this, he does not know many things. He does not know why he is now joyful, and he does not know the unification of "blessed be the name of the glory of His kingship for ever," and he does not know what the meat stew is in our sages' parable of "a princess who smelled a meat stew; if she says anything, it is shameful. If she does not say anything, she suffers (because of her desire for it—Rashi)" (*Pesachim* 56a), and he doesn't know the meaning of *chash* in *chashmal*,[7] and he doesn't know what is *nogah*, as in the verse, "and light (*nogah*) surrounded him" (Ezekiel 1:4), and he doesn't understand the Chariot, and he doesn't know what the covenant is, and he doesn't know why people are against him.

---

7. See *Likkutei Moharan* 1:82.

The messiah knows all this completely. The *tzaddikim* only know this when they turn the thousands into hundreds. Those *tzaddikim* who are "vengeful" and who can turn thousands into hundreds are a belt for the messiah. As our sages said, "If you see a Torah scholar who is 'vengeful' as a snake, tie him to your loins" – that is, a belt for the messiah, of which the verse says, "And justice will be tied to his loins" (Isaiah 11:5), which is translated in the Aramaic as "Just men – *tzaddikim* – will be around him," which is the level of "*matin, matin*" (*Berachot* 20a), meaning hundreds – that is, a person who can divide thousands into hundreds is a belt for the messiah. These great *tzaddikim* give life to the smaller *tzaddikim*.[8]

€€€

Faith in the *Tzaddik*

Once, Rabbi Nachman said that a person must strengthen his faith in the true *tzaddik* and grow so close to him that even after he dies his faith remains strong and no one can fool him.

After one's death, one still needs to be very strong in one's belief in the *tzaddik*.

There exist souls of evil people who oppose the *tzaddik*; these souls want to fool a person and keep him away from the true *tzaddik* in order to prevent him from being rectified.

But if a person remains strong in his faith, these forces will not be able to keep him from going to the *tzaddik* and receiving a rectification for his soul.

Even after one's death, one faces the obstacles of controversy and the like that confuse and fool one. The evil spirits speak badly about the *tzaddik* in order to weaken one's resolve to go to him.

(As long as a person has not come to his final resting place, he has not arrived at the world of truth. To the contrary, he is punished by destructive forces that lead him through the world of chaos, so that it appears to him that he is still in this world.)

8. Source: *Sichot Haran*, no. 93.

But if a person is strong and does not listen to them, if he says, "I am not going to listen to you, and I want to go to the *tzaddik*," these forces cannot hold him back.[9]

◄◄◄

The Journey of the Dead Merchant

Rabbi Nachman told that there was a man from Reisen (White Russia) who had traveled to the land of Israel together with the holy and well-known *tzaddik*, Rabbi Menachem Mendel of Vitebsk. It was decided that he would go to collect money for the Jews of the land of Israel, as is the custom.

While he was sailing, he died. Meanwhile, no one in the land of Israel knew of this.

After he died, he imagined that he was traveling to Leipzig with his servant and wagon driver to do business, as he had done during his lifetime, for he had been an important merchant.

On the way, he began to yearn to travel to Rabbi Menachem Mendel.

He wanted to put everything aside and turn back in the middle of the trip. But when he told his men what he intended to do, they began to make fun of him and to dissuade him. How could he consider losing this business? In this way, they kept him from going to Rabbi Menachem Mendel.

Afterward, he again had a great desire to go to his rabbi. Again, when he told his men, they dissuaded him. How could such a great merchant as he turn back from Leipzig and travel to his rabbi's house?

He listened to them again.

But afterward, he had a burning desire, and he declared, "I am not going to listen to you at all." He wanted very badly to set everything else aside and to travel to his rabbi.

The more his men dissuaded him, the more stubborn he grew, and he insisted that they travel to his rabbi right away.

---

9. Source: *Chayei Moharan* 1:46, no. 21.

He commanded them to turn back and travel with him to his rabbi.

When they saw that they could not dissuade him, they said that they would no longer follow his orders.

He insisted that they do what he said, but they refused.

He grew very angry at them. He was in charge and they had to listen to whatever he said.

Then they told him the truth: that he was already dead, and that they were destructive beings who were leading him about and fooling him.

He said, "Now I really insist that you take me to the *tzaddik* at once."

They said, "Now we really refuse," and they began to argue a legal case with him.

Finally, the case came to the highest court.

The court ruled that they must listen to him and take him immediately.

At once, they brought him to Rabbi Menachem Mendel of Vitebsk, who was still alive and in the land of Israel.

When this man entered the house of the *tzaddik*, one of the destructive angels entered with him, and the *tzaddik* was so frightened that he fainted.

After Rabbi Menachem Mendel was revived, he spent about eight days working on this man until he rectified him. He told the others that the messenger had died, for they still had not learned of it, and he told them the entire story.[10]

❄❄❄

How to Cling to the *Tzaddik*

Rabbi Nachman said that in order to be sure that one will come to the *tzaddik* after one's death, one should make an oath to this effect while holding a holy object.[11]

---

10. Source: *Chayei Moharan* 1:46, no. 21.
11. Source: *Chayei Moharan* 1:46, no. 21.

€€€

The Nonintellectual *Tzaddik*

It is possible to be a great *tzaddik* even if one hasn't learned
much.[12]

€€€

The *Tzaddik* and Trust in God

It is possible for someone to be a *tzaddik* even if his trust in God
isn't perfect.[13]

€€€

The Face of the *Tzaddik*

When one sees the face of the *tzaddik*, one's intellect is
sharpened.[14]

€€€

Attachment to the *Tzaddik*

It may be that years pass and one is not progressing in one's awe
of heaven, but remains on his original level or has even fallen.
Still, if he is close to the true *tzaddik*, this attachment itself is of
infinite value.[15]

---

12. Source: *Sefer Hamidot, Tzaddik*, no. 80.
13. Perhaps this is true because the *tzaddik*'s primary characteristic is his compassion.
Source: *Sefer Hamidot, Tzaddik*, no. 103.
14. Source: *Sefer Hamidot, Tzaddik*, no. 138.
15. Source: *Chayei Moharan* 2:19, no. 25.

€€€

The Field of Souls

There is a field in which grow extraordinarily beautiful trees and grasses. The extraordinary beauty of that field cannot be conveyed in words.

These trees and grasses are holy souls growing there.

Some souls are naked. They wander outside the field and wait for their rectification in order to be able to return to their place. Sometimes, even a great soul upon which other souls depend [through which other souls relate to Godliness] goes out of the field and finds it hard to return.

All of them look to the master of the field, who can work to rectify them.

There is a soul that is rectified by the death of a person, or by someone else's *mitzvah* and worship.

Whoever desires to gird his loins and to enter and be the master of the field must be a powerful warrior, a broad-shouldered man, and a very great *tzaddik*. He must be an extraordinary human being.

Some people can only reach this level with their death. Even to reach such a level, one must be very great. There are many great people who will not reach this level even with their death.

Only a person on an extraordinarily high level can accomplish all that he needs to in his lifetime. He must suffer many troubles and difficult experiences. But on his great level, he passes through all these experiences and he labors in the field as is necessary. Then, when he manages to rectify the souls and to bring them back into the field, [they] can pray, for prayer has then been rectified.

This master of the field is in charge of constantly watering the trees and growing them, as well as tending to the other needs of the field. He keeps the trees at a proper distance from each other, so that they do not weaken each other. Sometimes, one must act distantly to a disciple, in order that the disciple will not crush his fellow.

When the eyes of the master of the field shine, he can look at every individual and see if that individual is close to the ultimate purpose. When someone is distant from the ultimate purpose, that person's prayer is not yet perfect, for he cannot make his entire prayer into a oneness. When he finishes saying a word, he has already forgotten the beginning of the word, and he cannot integrate his prayer into oneness.

The master of the field gazes upon him and brings him to the ultimate purpose, which is entirely one.[16]

❧❧❧

Vision of the Man in the Circle

I will tell you what I saw. And you tell your children.

Someone was lying on the ground, and people sat about him in a circle. There was a second circle around the first, a third circle, and so on.

Around these circles sat some other people in no particular order.

The man who was sitting in the middle on his side was moving his lips, and everyone around him moved his lips like him.

Then I saw that the man in the middle was no longer there, and all the people sitting about him stopped moving their lips.

"What is going on?" I asked.

I was told that the man had grown cold and died. Since he had ceased to speak, the others had ceased to speak as well.

Afterward, everyone began running.

I ran after them. I saw two beautiful palaces.

Two ministers sat there.

The people ran to the ministers and began to complain to them, "Why did you fool us?" They wanted to kill the ministers. Finally, the ministers ran out.

When I saw the ministers, I very much liked them. I ran after them.

From afar, I saw a beautiful tent.

---

16. Source: *Likkutei Moharan* 1:65:1.

People shouted from there to the minsters, "Go back! Find all your merits. Take them in your hand and go to the candle that is hanging there. There you will be able to accomplish all that you want."

The ministers went back and took their merits. There were bundles of merits. They ran to the candle, and I ran after them.

A lit candle was hanging in the air. The ministers came and threw the merits at the candle, and sparks fell from the candle into their mouths.

The candle turned into a river,[17] and everyone drank from it.

Creatures were formed within them. When they opened their mouths to speak, the creatures emerged.

I saw these running back and forth. They were neither human nor animal – just creatures.

Afterward, the ministers decided to return to their place.

They said, "How can we get back to our place?"

One of them said, "Let us send a message to the person who is standing there and holding a sword from the heaven to the earth."

They said, "Whom shall we send?"

They decided to send the creatures. The creatures went there, and I ran after them.

I saw a frightening being standing from heaven to the earth with a sword in his hand that reached from heaven to earth and that had many blades.

One blade was sharp for killing; another blade was for poverty; another blade was for weakness. And there were a number of other blades for other punishments.

They began, "It is a long time that we have suffered because of you. Now help us and bring us to our place."

He said, "I cannot help you."

They asked, "Give us the blade of death and we will kill the people."

But he did not agree.

They asked for another blade, but he did not want to give them any blade. So they left.

---

17. The words *the candle* and *river* have the same letters.

Meanwhile, an order was given to kill the ministers, and their heads were cut off.

Then things went back to what they had been previously.

A person lay on the ground and there were circles of people about him, and they ran to the ministers, and so forth, all over again.

But this time, I saw that the ministers did not throw their merits at the candle. Instead, they took the merits, went to the candle, broke their hearts, and began to beg before the candle. Sparks fell from the candle into their mouths.

They pleaded more and the candle turned into a river, and so on, and the creatures were formed. And I was told, "These will live. The first ones were guilty of death because they threw the merits at the candle and did not plead, as these had."

I didn't understand this.

I was told, "Go to a certain room and you will be told what it all means."

I went there, and an old man was sitting there. I asked him about this.

He grasped his beard and told me, "This beard is the explanation of the story."

I answered him, "I still don't understand."

He told me, "Go to such and such a room, and there you will find the explanation."

I went there, and I saw a long, broad, endless room, full of writings. And every place that I opened, I saw an explanation of the story.

Rabbi Nosson heard this directly from Rabbi Nachman. Rabbi Nachman said that all his teachings contain hints about this story. And the teaching in *Likkutei Moharan*, "Nine Rectifications" (no. 20), is in its entirety a commentary on this story.[18]

€€€

So Far from the *Tzaddik*

Rabbi Nachman told us that he had had a dream and he didn't know what it meant.

18. Source: *Chayei Moharan* 1:36, no. 2.

One of my disciples had died (someone who had actually died). But I hadn't known about it until now.

It seemed to me that everyone was standing around me and taking leave of me after Rosh Hashanah, as is the custom.

That man who had died was also standing there. I asked him, "Why weren't you here on Rosh Hashanah?"

The man answered, "Hadn't I already died?"

I replied, "Is that a reason? If a man dies, isn't he allowed to come for Rosh Hashanah?"

And the man was silent.

Because a few people were speaking with me about faith, I also spoke with him about this. (Apparently, Rabbi Nachman understood that this man had had problems with his faith [in the *tzaddik*].)

I told him, "Am I the only one in the world? If you don't believe in me, go to other *tzaddikim*. Since you still believe in others, go to them."

He said, "Whom shall I go to?"

I think that I told him to go to some well-known leader.

He answered, "I am far from him."

I told him, "Go to some other one." I mentioned all the famous leaders. But he said that he was far from every one of them.

I told him, "Since you are far from all of them and you have no one to approach, you should stay here and grow close to me."

"To you?" he said. "From you I am really very far!"

I believe that it was mid-day, and the sun was directly overhead. The man rose up into the air until he reached the sun. He traveled with the sun and they sank bit by bit to the ground together, until he sank below the earth together with sunset.

He continued with the sun until midnight, when he was directly below me, for at midnight the sun is directly below a person's feet.

Then, when he had sunk far down until he was directly opposite me, I heard a cry calling to me, "Do you hear how far I am from you?"

And I do not know what this means.[19]

---

19. Source: *Chayei Moharan* 1:46, no. 21.

❧❧❧

A *Tzaddik* Can Err

At times, strict judgments emerge into this world and enter the leaders of the generation, precisely because these leaders have great knowledge. These strict judgments enter the awareness of the leaders and then come out through their mouths in the form of words.

These words are on the level of strict judgments, and the person to whom they occurred must attempt to ameliorate them.

But he may not be able to do so. Possibly, he does not have the requisite power. Alternatively, he may be on a temporarily low plane, due to having committed some error or sin. Even *tzaddikim* and leaders at times commit errors, for "there is no righteous man [*tzaddik*] in the world [who does good and never sins]" (Ecclesiastes 7:20). Since he is on that level, he cannot ameliorate the strict judgments, which are the words. Then such a leader begins to speak evil words in general or in particular, or he speaks against the *tzaddik* of the generation. Then all of his words, which are strict judgments, come and fall upon the *tzaddik* of the generation, who then has the task of ameliorating those strict judgments.[20]

❧❧❧

The Doctrine of the *Tzaddik*

The foundation on which everything rests is connecting oneself to the *tzaddik* of the generation and accepting whatever he says as authoritative, whether it be a minor or a major matter. One should not turn from his words either to the right or to the left.

---

20. It is not clear from here, however, whether the singular *tzaddik* of the generation is himself liable to error.

Source: *Likkutei Moharan* 1:207.

As our rabbis said (*Sifri, Shoftim*), "Even if they tell you right is left, do not turn aside from their command."

One must cast aside all intellectual accomplishments and remove one's consciousness, as though one has no intellect besides what one receives from the *tzaddik* and teacher of the generation.

As long as one still has one's own intellect, one is not perfected and still not connected to the *tzaddik*.

At the time that the people of Israel received the Torah, they had great wisdoms. In their day, there were idol worshipers whose error was a result of great wisdom and philosophy.

If the Jews hadn't cast aside those wisdoms, they would not have received the Torah. They would have been able to deny everything, God forbid, and nothing that Moses did for them would have helped. Not even all the awesome miracles that he performed before their eyes would have helped them. Even today, heretics deny Torah using the folly of their cleverness.

But Israel, being a holy nation, saw the truth. They cast aside their wisdom and believed in God and in Moses His servant. As a result, they received the Torah.

The Aramaic translation of the Pentateuch, Onkelos, renders "A foolish nation and not wise" (Deuteronomy 32:6) as "a nation that received the Torah and did not grow wise." In other words, they received the Torah because they "did not grow wise" – they cast aside all their wisdom [before Torah, which is the highest wisdom].[21]

---

21. Rabbi Nachman tells us that he is about to say what the foundation of Judaism is. One might expect a statement on the belief in one God. Instead, he says that the foundation is to bind oneself to the *tzaddik* of the generation.

He then interprets a statement from the Talmud to mean that whatever a *tzaddik* says must be assumed to be true, even if it violates common sense. In context, the Talmud's statement refers specifically to legal decisions. No matter how much one disagrees with a legal decision of the rabbis, one is duty-bound to accept it. The classic twelfth-century *Sefer Hachinuch* comments, "Even if [the ruling rabbis] will err regarding a particular matter, we must act in accordance with their error, for it is better to suffer one error and have everyone accepting [the rabbis'] correct interpretations always, rather than every individual doing as he thinks correct; for that would destroy the religion, divide the heart of the people, and ruin the nation completely" (commandment 496). One has the right to disagree with a rabbi's ruling, but, as in any legal system, one is duty-bound to accept it.

But Rabbi Nachman states that as long as one retains one's own intellect, one is not yet perfected and connected to the *tzaddik*.

Rabbi Nachman then explains that the Jews were able to accept the Torah only as a result of casting off all wisdoms. Rabbi Moshe Isserles, the great codifer of Jewish law of sixteenth-century Cracow, seems to have viewed the matter differently. He wrote that "during the forty-nine days after leaving Egypt until the giving of the Torah, the [Jews] learned all the wisdoms of the philosophers and the nature of created phenomena. As a result, they were prepared for prophecy at the time of the giving of the Torah, each according to the level that he had previously attained." According to this, it was not as a result of casting away non-Jewish thought, but rather of learning secular wisdom, that the Jews were prepared to receive the Torah.

Regarding such controversies, the Talmud states, "Both opinions are the words of the living God" (*Gittin* 6b)—what appears to us to be irreconcilable differences are actually different expressions of Godly truth.

Rabbi Nachman is not calling for uncritical acceptance of any authority figure. This is clear from his teachings disparaging false and unfit leaders. A true *tzaddik* must prove himself to the potential disciple by fulfilling certain conditions. He must, for instance, be very learned in Torah, have a reputation among other leaders for piety, demonstrate an ability to awaken others to develop their spiritual potential, and so on. One is required to use his critical perceptions when choosing a *tzaddik*.

Rabbi Nachman says that a person must find the *tzaddik* of the generation. In several places, Rabbi Nachman points out that the *tzaddik* of the generation is in a sense on the level of Moses, quoting a statement from the Talmud that the rabbis used to call each other Moses.

This is odd, because there was only one Moses, but there are many rabbis.

One can say, therefore, that there can be more than one Moses living at a time. Each such leader creates or expresses a spiritual reality that is an entire universe to itself. Just as present-day physicists posit simultaneous alternate universes, so within this physical world are there separate *tzaddikim* drawing down into the world different spiritual universes. Thus, each *tzaddik* is indeed the leader of the entire world.

Two *tzaddikim* can live together, and even vigorously disagree, yet both are the one *tzaddik* of the generation. Spirituality is a level that transcends time and space. Only where time and space exist is such a statement a paradox.

One must find one's own Moses. One must find him not only out there, but also within one's heart, forging a deep internal connection with him.

One must find a teacher based on a sense that this teacher is the spokesman for one's soul, can see things that escape one, and can guide one in ways that one perhaps does not understand, but that one always eventually finds nurturing. In this sense, a *tzaddik* is analogous to a psychotherapist. The patient must accept the authority of the psycho-therapist, at least in a limited sense, precisely because the therapist is not acting in an authoritarian manner but is working to bring out the latent strengths of the patient's personality. When a *tzaddik* has demonstrated such a level of ability, and one has formed an intimate bond with him as a mature, separate human being, then one accepts his authority even if it doesn't make sense at the moment. This is not blind faith; the *tzaddik* has already demonstrated his reliability.

In one sense, one retains one's critical faculties; one learns the sciences to prepare for the receiving of the Torah, as per Rabbi Isserles. Yet in another sense, this no longer constitutes one's paradigm of reality – instead, it has become a tool of another paradigm: that of a trustworthy, intimate relationship with one's true spiritual leader.

Rabbi Nachman a number of times quotes the saying, "There cannot be a king without a nation" (*Kad Hakemach, Rosh Hashanah* 70a). A person cannot be a *tzaddik* without followers. Does this mean that a *tzaddik* without followers is not a *tzaddik*? This doesn't seem to make sense – even if a great musician didn't have listeners, that would not detract from his independent greatness.

Perhaps the statement can be interpreted as follows: the greatness of a *tzaddik* is that he affects and transforms others. If he does not transform others, then he is not a *tzaddik*. This is not analogous to a musician and his audience but, rather, to a musician and his instru-ment. "There cannot be a pianist without a piano."

The statement mentions that the king needs the nation, not that the nation needs the king. Perhaps this means that, in fact, a person can

€€€

Tzaddik and Disciple

Rabbi Nachman also told me, "Without me, you cannot do anything. But without you, I cannot do anything either."[22]

live independent of a spiritual master – but he must first be on the level of a nation. A nation is characterized by being a civilization.

As a first step, a person must be civilized – he must have good personality traits. Only then does he look to perfect his spirituality. Therefore, the person is already independent. He does not go to a tzaddik as an authoritarian master to whom he will give over his sense of self. Only a person who has previously denied his sense of self-worth is susceptible to such a temptation. Rather, a person who is on the level of being civilized, of having a strong sense of self, goes to the tzaddik. He retains his strong sense of self as a personality, even as he gives the tzaddik authority to help him perfect his spiritual self.

Thus, each person must pick the tzaddik that will best develop his spiritual self. Each person must pick the tzaddik of the generation who is best suited for him, rather than trying to recast himself to fit a person who he thinks "should" be his spiritual master. Thus, there can be various "tzaddikim of the generation"; more than that, some of them may be alive and some may actually be from previous generations. A person may choose various spiritual masters. Although he may look to one of them as his central teacher, he may have a spectrum of different teachers, living and not living, including teachers who either apparently or actually disagree with each other.

One can go further. As Rabbi Nachman points out, the Zohar indicates the identification between the messiah and Moses – that is, that they both share the same soul, at least to some extent. If that is the case, and if every tzaddik of the generation is called Moses, then every tzaddik of the generation contains within himself a spark or splinter of the soul of Moses. In a sense, all the different tzaddikim of the generation are actually aspects of the same person, of the same messianic personality.

Source: *Likkutei Moharan* 1:123.
22. Source: *Chayei Moharan* 2:21, no. 40.

16

Rabbi Nachman

The Beautiful Tree

I am a beautiful, wonderful tree with wonderful branches, and below I am literally in the depths of the earth.[1]

€€€

Miracles: A Minor Matter

We do not spend time telling the awesome miracles that we saw Rabbi Nachman perform. In comparison with the great levels that he reached, he did not regard this as praise. Instead, we have told that which is relevant to serving God, in order to awaken the desire of the wise person. There are no excuses. Every person can achieve the highest levels if he will go in the path of Rabbi Nachman.[2]

---

1. Source: *Chayei Moharan* 2:8, no. 5.
2. Source: *Shivhei Haran*, no. 27.

≪≪≪

The New Path That Is Really Old

Rabbi Nachman said, "Pray for me that I may recover from my disease and lead you on a new path that never before existed, even though it is really an old path."[3]

≪≪≪

Rabbi Nachman's Humility

Rabbi Nachman said, "I am more humble than any other leader. Everyone has his service, but I am humble. Others do not measure up to me at all, for the trait of modesty is to be absolutely nothing in one's own eyes. Since they are nothing compared to me, I am their humility.

"Of all the well-known leaders, I am the humble one. One leader does one thing and another does another, but I do not hold them to be anything. By combining them all, I have the trait of modesty among them. But whom do I hold to be most of a nothing—I or they?" It appeared that he held himself to be more of a nothing.[4]

≪≪≪

There Is No Middle Ground

Many times, Rabbi Nachman quoted the popular statement that people were making about him that there is no middle ground here. Either Rabbi Nachman is what his opponents claim he is, or he is a wondrous, awesome, unique *tzaddik* whom no human mind can fathom.

---

3. Source: *Chayei Moharan* 2:11, no. 24.
4. Source: *Chayei Moharan* 2:12, no. 29.

He repeated these words many times and hinted to us that indeed there is no middle ground.[5]

❈❈❈

No One Knows Him

Rabbi Nachman said, "Just as those who are against me don't know who I am, neither do those who support me know who I am, except Nosson and Naftali, a little bit."[6]

❈❈❈

Unique

Once, Rabbi Nachman was sitting together with a holy rabbi—possibly the preacher of Terhavitza—at *seudah shlishit* on Shabbat. He grasped the beard of the preacher in a friendly way and told him, "There has never before been a unique figure like me."[7]

❈❈❈

The World Could Not Exist

Once Rabbi Nachman said, "The world should plead for me, for it needs me a great deal, and it could not exist without me."[8]

❈❈❈

---

5. Source: *Chayei Moharan* 2:10, no. 22.
6. Source: *Avanehah Barzel*, p. 24.
7. Source: *Chayei Moharan* 2:9, no. 7.
8. Source: *Chayei Moharan* 2:10, no. 8.

An Extraordinary Soul

Rabbi Nachman said, "I am an extraordinary man, and my soul is very extraordinary."[9]

⋙

Leader of the Young

Once, Rabbi Nachman said, "I used to think that it was my evil inclination that was telling me that no one can lead young people as I can. Now I know clearly that I am the only leader of the generation, and there is no other leader like me."[10]

⋙

Take Advantage

He told me, "There will be a time when you deeply regret that you had such an extraordinarily unique person among you and you didn't take advantage of him."[11]

⋙

Hidden Joy of the Laboring *Tzaddik*

Rabbi Nachman said, "You do not have to learn from my revealed aspect. Even though I usually appear to be depressed, you do not have to learn from this. You should be constantly joyful. I too am really joyful. But I have to continuously blaze a path through a desert waste and cut away all the barriers. I must cut down great trees that are thousands of years old, and go back and forth, cutting down again and again, in order that the path

---

9. Source: *Chayei Moharan* 2:10, no. 16.
10. Source: *Chayei Moharan* 2:10, no. 18.
11. Source: *Chayei Moharan* 2:10, no. 19.

will be fit for the masses, so that they will be able to go on that road." Because of those exertions, he was usually worried.

Rabbi Nachman said that [his student] Rabbi Shimon is also involved in clearing the road.[12]

❦❦❦

King David and the Broken Heart

We also heard that Rabbi Nachman's family is descended from King David, as is well known, and such people usually go about with a broken heart and do not have happy faces. This is because King David is the founder of the Book of Psalms, which is primarily composed of words that come from a broken heart. All of King David's words are nothing but cries and pleas from a deeply broken heart. His offspring also now usually have a broken heart.

But Rabbi Nachman admonished us to be joyful constantly.[13]

❦❦❦

Rabbi Nachman's Throne

"On the throne [or chair] was the image of a man, above it" (Ezekiel 1:26) [referring to Ezekiel's vision of the Divine Presence]. Rabbi Nachman once grasped the two arms of his chair and rocked back and forth, saying with great awe, "When one sits upon a chair, then one is a man."

And these matters are deeply hidden.[14]

❦❦❦

Rabbi Nachman's Work

Rabbi Nachman said, "I have such an understanding of God that I could have used it to bring the messiah. But I cast everything

---

12. Source: *Chayei Moharan* 2:6, no. 16.
13. Source: *Chayei Moharan* 2:6, no. 7.
14. Source: *Chayei Moharan* 1:7, no. 2.

aside and dedicated myself to you, to improve you, for this is the greatest thing of all. Fortunate is the man who takes the hand of the sinner."

He admonished his followers a great deal and told them, "I worked terribly hard for you. Many times, my throat was dried out because of all my prayers regarding each one of you. And now, what have I accomplished? Even though you are all kosher people, this is not what I had wanted.[15] How will I come before the throne of glory? But I console myself a bit with my followers who are already in the world-to-come"—that is, those followers who had already passed away, since they were definitely His disciples, whereas those who are alive are still in great danger.[16]

⋘

Rabbi Nachman and the Messiah

Rabbi Nachman said, "All the good things that the messiah will do for the Jews, I can do. The only difference is that the messiah can decree and bring things about, whereas I . . ."—and he paused and didn't continue. According to another version, he continued, "But I still cannot bring things to completion."[17]

⋘

Rabbi Nachman's Accomplishment

I (Rabbi Nosson) once asked Rabbi Nachman, "What will happen of all that we had spoken?" We had at first heard him say a number of things that indicated that he would live a long time and complete his task.

He answered, "Did you hear what he's asking? This is also

---

15. It is known that he had wanted to make us all extraordinarily high *tzaddikim*.

16. Source: *Chayei Moharan* 2:10, no. 17.

17. Source: *Chayei Moharan* 2:12, no. 26.

difficult for me [to understand]." Still, he said, "Didn't I complete it? I have already accomplished, and I will still accomplish!"

When Rabbi Nachman traveled to Uman with me, he spoke to me about the idea that God is constantly accomplishing. All the paper in the world would not suffice to explain all these matters.

At first, he had thought that when we drew close to him that he would bring about the rectification immediately. But then, due to our sins, the sins of the generation, and the great opposition of the evil spirit, which caused the great controversy, the world was confused and he couldn't complete what he had wanted to in his lifetime. But he said that he did accomplish and he would accomplish, for after he returned from Lemberg, he had attained such a path and he spoke such words that his candle would never go out.

He said, "My fire will burn until the messiah comes."[18]

---

18. Source: *Chayei Moharan* 1:90, no. 44.

17

Bratslav *Chasidim*

The Signs of a Bratslav *Chasid*

Rabbi Nachman once said, "I have succeeded in three things with God:

1. I have broken your egoism. When you pray, people will say, "That is a Bratslaver *chasid*."

2. Committing a sin will make you sick. You won't be able to accomplish it, either. Even if you do it, it will be without hands and feet.

3. You won't even be able to look at false leaders, for you have already tasted the real Hungarian wine."[1]

€€€

The Whole World Will Be Bratslav

Rabbi Nachman said that in the future, the whole world would be comprised of Bratslav *chasidim*.

---

1. Source: *Avanehah Barzel*, p. 28.

We learn in the *midrash* (*Bereshit Rabbah* 34:21) on the verse, "I have given you a heart of flesh" (Ezekiel 36:26): "Do not read 'flesh'—*basar*—but 'not desiring'—*boser*; everyone will be satisfied with his own portion and not desire the portion of his fellow." "Heart that doesn't desire" has the same letters as "Bratslav."[2]

2. Source: *Chayei Moharan* 2:23, no. 49.

18

Camaraderie

The King and the Bird

Once there was a king who was also an astrologer. He saw that
if the wheat was not cut by a certain time, it would all get ruined.
There was very little time. He decided to take harvesters and to
give them all sorts of pleasures and everything they needed so
that they would have the state of mind to work day and night and
cut the grain on time.

But they grew so happy that they forgot. Time passed; they
didn't cut the wheat, and it was all ruined.

They knew that the king would be angry at them, and they
didn't know what to do.

A wise man told them that the king loves a certain bird. This
man advised them that if they brought the king the bird, he
would have so much delight and pleasure in it that he would
forgive them everything.

It was very difficult to catch the bird, because it was very high
up in the air. The people had no ladder, and the time was short.

The wise man advised them that since they are many, they

111

should form a human ladder, one person standing on top of the other, until they reached the bird.

But the people fought with each other, because everyone wanted to be on top with the other one below him.

Because of their argument, they grew careless, and the bird flew away.

As a result, they were left with the king's anger at them for being careless and not cutting the wheat.[1]

❮❮❮

The Direct Light and the Reflected Light

When one speaks with a friend about serving God, one's words are like a light. The reaction from one's friend is like a reflected light.

Sometimes, the reflected light precedes the direct light. If one's friend is in a small state of consciousness and is unable to receive one's words, then one receives the reflected light before he receives the direct light.

When one speaks with one's friend about serving God, even if he doesn't understand, one nevertheless receives an enthusiasm in return. The light is reflected back from one's friend. This is like bouncing an object against a wall. Even if one's friend doesn't understand, one can be woken by one's own words, by the reflected light. If one had spoken these words to oneself, it is possible that they wouldn't have had any effect. But since one spoke them to someone else, one was woken, even if the other person was not, for the words were reflected back.[2]

1. Source: *Kochavei Ohr*, p. 28.
2. Source: *Likkutei Moharan* 1:184.

19

False Leaders

Praying for the Sake of a Cat

Once, Rabbi Nachman told his daughter, Adil, about a well-known leader who had for nine years prayed with great intensity because a cat scratched outside his door, and he thought that his *Chasidim* were pushing each other to listen to him. When he learned the truth, he realized that he had been praying for the sake of the cat.[1]

€€€

Agents of the Angel of Death

Rabbi Nachman said that it would be too difficult for the angel of death to kill everyone, whether physically or spiritually.

Therefore, he took helpers: doctors to kill people physically, and false leaders to kill them spiritually.

Rabbi Nachman said, "If the doctors sometimes heal someone, it is only like a bandage on a wound."

---

1. Source: *Avanehah Barzel*, p. 25.

113

He also said, "There are two types of people that I am afraid
of: a[n anti-Semitic] Gentile and a false *tzaddik*. They have no
idea how great their power is. If they would know, they would be
even worse, God save us."[2]

2. Source: *Avanehah Barzel*, p. 43.

20

Self-Renewal

It Is Not Good to Be Old

It is not good to be old—neither an old *Chasid*, nor an old *tzaddik*. Being old is not good.

One must renew oneself every day; one must begin at every moment.[1]

❦❦❦

The Beggar Who Was Very Old and Very Young

"Here I am," the blind beggar called out to the young, newlywed couple. "When I came to your wedding, I wished you to be as old as I am. But today I am giving this to you as an outright gift.

"You think that I am blind. I am not blind at all. But to me, all the time of the world is not worth an eye blink." (That is, he

---

1. Source: *Sichot Haran*, no. 51.

115

appears to be blind because he does not look at the world, for the entire world is not worth an eye blink to him.)

"I am very old, but I am very young. And I have not even begun to live. Yet I am very old.

"And not only I say this, but I have testimony to this effect from the great eagle.

"I will tell you a story:

"Once, people sailed on the sea on many ships. A storm came and broke the ships. The people were saved, and they went to a tower. When they entered the tower, they found all sorts of food, drink, clothing, and whatever else they needed. They had everything good there, all the pleasures in the world.

"They decided that everyone should tell an old story that he called from his earliest memory.

"There were young and old people there. They asked the oldest person among them to speak first.

"He said to them, 'What shall I tell you? I remember when the apple was cut from the branch.'

"No one understood what he meant.

"But the wise men who were there said, 'Indeed, this is a very old story.'

"The next-oldest man then spoke. 'Is that an old story?' he said. 'I remember that, and I also remember when the light was burning.'

"The people exclaimed, 'This is an even older story than the first one!'

"They were very surprised that the second man should recall an older story than the first man did.

"Then they asked the third-oldest man to speak.

"He said, 'I even remember when the fruit began to form and became a fruit.'

"The people said, 'This story is even older.'

"Then the fourth oldest man spoke. 'I even remember when the seed was planted to form the fruit.'

"The fifth-oldest man said, 'I even remember the wise men who thought up the seed.'

"The sixth-oldest man said, 'I even remember the taste of the fruit before the taste entered the fruit'.

"The seventh man then said, 'I even remember the fragrance of the fruit before the fragrance entered the fruit.'

"The eighth man then said, 'I even remember the appearance of the fruit before the appearance entered the fruit.'

"I was there as well – at that time, I was still a child. I said, 'I remember all these stories, and I remember nothing.'

"The people said, 'This is a very old story, the oldest of them all.'

"They were very surprised that this child remembers more than anyone else.

"Meanwhile, the great eagle came, and knocked at the tower.

"He told the people, 'Stop being poor. Return to your riches! Use your wealth!' He promised them that they would leave the tower in order of age, the oldest leaving first.

"He took them all out of the tower.

"He first called me out, because I was really the oldest of them all. He took the youngest ones out first, and he took out the oldest man last; for whoever was younger was older (and thus remembered the older story).

"The oldest man was the youngest of them all.

"The great eagle said to them, 'I will explain to you all of the stories that everyone told.

" 'One person told that he still remembers when the apple was cut from the branch. He means that he even remembers when his umbilical cord was cut.

" 'The next man, who told that he even remembers when the light was burning, means that he remembers when he was a fetus, where a light shone over his head (for the Talmud tells that when the child is in the mother's belly, a light shines over his head).

" 'The person who told that he remembers when the fruit began to form means that he remembers when his body began to form.

" 'The one who remembers when the seed was brought to plant the fruit means that he remembers how the drop of semen was drawn down.

" 'The man who remembers the wise men who thought up the

seed means that he remembers when the drop of semen was still in the mind.

" 'The man who remembers the taste – that is the *nefesh*, the soul's lowest level.

" 'He who remembers the fragrance – this is the *ruach*, the soul's middle level.

" 'And the appearance – this is the *neshamah*, the soul's upper level.

" 'The child who said that he remembers nothing is greater than all of them. He remembers even what existed before these three levels of the soul.

" 'That is why he said that he remembers nothing – he remembers when nothing existed, which is the very highest level.'

"The great eagle told the people, 'Go back to your ships. They are your bodies that were broken. They will be rebuilt. Today, go back to them.'

"And he blessed them.

"And to me, the blind beggar, he said, 'You come with me, because you are like me. Like me, you are very old and very young. You have not even begun to live, but you are nevertheless very old. And I am the same, for I too am very old and yet very young.'

"So I have the testimony of the great eagle that I am both very old and very young, and everything else that I mentioned.

"Today I give you an outright wedding gift that you should be as old as I am."

There was great joy there, and they were very happy.[2]

---

2. Source: *Sippurei Maasiyot*, "The Seven Beggars," p. 198.

21

Prayer

With Prayer, One Can Achieve Everything

Someone asked Rabbi Nachman how to come close to God.
Rabbi Nachman told him to learn Torah.

"But I do not know how to learn."

Rabbi Nachman answered that with prayer one can achieve
everything: Torah, service of God, all levels of holiness, and all
the goodness in the world.

Once, Rabbi Nachman said, "If a dead person were allowed to
return to this world and pray, you can be sure that he would pray
with all his might."[1]

⋘

Praying with Strength

Rabbi Nachman admonished us strongly to put all our strength
into the words of prayer.

---

1. Source: *Likkutei Moharan* 2:111.

He said that a person must force himself a great deal when he prays. A minority opinion holds that a person shouldn't force himself in prayer. But this is not right—a person must force himself with all his strength when he prays.

Rabbi Nachman also said that when a person prays with feeling—that is, when he connects his thoughts to the words, paying attention and listening to what he is saying—his strength is automatically drawn into the words of prayer. This is because a person's strength automatically waits and looks to be drawn into holy words.

When a person prays with feeling, all his powers are drawn into his prayer. Then he prays with great strength, even though he isn't forcing himself.[2]

❊❊❊

The Simple Meaning

Rabbi Nachman didn't recommend that people pray with the meditative intentions of the *Ari*—not even those people who were on his recommendation learning the writings of the *Ari*. He said that the essence of perfected prayer is the simple meaning of the words. One should have in mind the meaning of the words, and one should hear what one is saying.[3]

❊❊❊

Meditations

The only people who should pray with the kabbalistic, meditative intentions of the *Ari* are those who understand those meditative intentions to such a degree that the meditations comprise the simple meaning of the words. This is the level of the great, true *tzaddikim*. If a person is not on this level, he should only have in mind the simple meaning of the words.[4]

---

2. Source: *Sichot Haran*, no. 66.
3. Source: *Sichot Haran*, no. 75.
4. Source: *Likkutei Eitzot*, Prayer, no. 94.

22

Hitbodedut Meditation

What is *Hitbodedut?*

The practice of *hitbodedut* is on a very great level. It is higher than everything else.

One practices *hitbodedut* as follows: one sets aside at least one hour, if not more, to be alone in a room or in a field, and one speaks extemporaneously to God, with pleading, words of grace, requests for acceptance and forgiveness, beseeching God to draw one to truly serve Him.

This prayer should be in one's native tongue, and not, as the formal prayers are, in Hebrew. This is because unless Hebrew is one's native tongue, it is difficult to speak one's mind in the Holy Tongue. One's heart isn't drawn after the words, because one isn't used to that language. But in one's native tongue, it is easier to affect oneself and break one's heart.

This is because the heart is affected by words in one's native tongue.

In one's native tongue, one can express oneself and tell God all that is in one's heart, whether it be regret and repentance for the past or a prayerful request to come close to God from this day forth, or other matters – each individual according to the level he is on.

One must do this every day for an hour.

For the rest of the day, one should be joyous.

This practice is on an extremely high level. It is a very good path by which to come close to God. It is a practice that includes everything else. Whatever one's imperfections, or [even] if one is completely removed from serving God, one can speak and plead before God.

Even if at times one's way is blocked and one cannot open one's mouth to speak to God, the very fact that one has prepared oneself to stand before God and that one desires to speak is itself very good.

One can turn this itself into a prayer. One can cry to God that one is so far from Him that one finds it impossible even to speak to Him. One can ask God for compassion to open one's mouth to speak to Him.

Many great and well-known *tzaddikim* reported that they only came to their level as a result of this practice.

The wise person will understand the greatness of this practice, which rises to the very heights.

This is a practice that anyone, great or small, can engage in. Everyone can do this and come to a great level.

Fortunate is the one who engages in this practice.[1]

---

1. Nominal Jewish expression of the heart is for the most part limited to prearranged prayers that one recites in Hebrew, among a quorum of other Jews. One must bring the feelings of one's heart into those words or, at a few standard parts in the prayer, insert a small prayer of one's own. In addition, one can read psalms.

A Jew on a more sophisticated spiritual level might use the prayer book as a meditative structure, using the words for mystical mental processes based primarily on the teachings of the *Ari*.

An extraordinarily pious Jew might engage in other, lone meditative practices, which were often dangerous to the imperfectly initiated.

In previous years, it was relatively common for Jews to compose their own spontaneous prayers. But generally speaking, these were occasional and the practice not systematized.

Rabbi Nachman offered a powerful system of meditation and approach to God that would be entirely safe and work for any individual to the full extent of his capabilities, even as the technique stretched those capabilities.

Furthermore, Rabbi Nachman's system does not require the individual to mold his psyche to a prearranged prayer or meditation, but rather offers a structure in which one can spontaneously and organically deal with the specific issues in one's life.

In this regard, *hitbodedut* bears resemblance to psychotherapy, in which a patient deals with the issues in his life as they come up.

The practice of *hitbodedut* reflects the idea that what is important in serving God is not intellectual or mystical accomplishment, but rather connecting to God in a direct, affective way. Even though one's *hitbodedut* may be on a simple level, it is no less meaningful, for it leads one to experience a profound sense of closeness to God and belief in His providence.

Hitbodedut is a spontaneous and unstructured meditative practice that needs no preparation or training. The practitioner of *hitbodedut* is not confined to a particular stance, chant, or ritualized set of movements. Thus, *hitbodedut* has two great advantages:

1. *Hitbodedut* doesn't stifle an individual by requiring him to maintain a rigid posture for long periods of time, to concentrate on one small object or one topic, or to maintain a certain level of meditative consciousness. Rather, it allows free mental and physical movement. This frees the practitioner to naturally and spontaneously deal with whatever particular part of his psyche needs correction, not forcing him to one limited area. It allows a person to let a great amount of illumination flow through him. He can help channel and dissipate the energy in any way he likes–dancing, clapping, singing, and so on.

2. It doesn't force a person to push himself to reach a goal that he isn't prepared to get to at the moment. *Hitbodedut* allows a person to develop his spiritual capacity at a natural pace.

Also, *hitbodedut* doesn't degenerate into a narcissistic fascination with one's own spiritual experience. *Hitbodedut* concentrates not on making oneself feel "high" but on establishing a connection with God and on achieving improvement in all areas of one's life.

Hitbodedut allows a person to act normally–to talk to God in a normal way, or sing, or clap and dance, or walk about, or plead, or argue, or review, the past, or speak of the future, and so on. *Hitbo-*

❡❡❡

A New Path

All the destructive forces already know about the written
prayers and lay in wait on the path of those prayers. This is like
a main road that everyone knows about, where murderers and
thieves lie in wait. But when one goes on a new path that is still
not known, they do not know to lie in wait there.

The same holds true for *hitbodedut*.

One's spontaneous speech with God is a new path and a new
prayer that a person creates from his heart.

Therefore, the negative forces aren't there to such an extent to
ambush him.

---

dedut does not stifle the intellect. A person can use his intellect in
speaking to God in examining his situation, even arguing with God, and
the like.

As a result, *hitbodedut* is particularly effective in (1) bringing
Godliness down into the practitioner and (2) extending this awareness
of God and of one's relationship to God into other areas of life.

In *hitbodedut* a person must speak, must move his lips and tongue,
must speak like a human being. He brings holiness down into his very
speaking and so into this world, rather than climbing up into a realm of
meditative silence. This applies to all the other spontaneous acts one
can carry out in *hitbodedut*.

Hitbodedut allows a person to begin with himself as he is.

A person can use *hitbodedut* to deal with whatever is on his mind,
from the most personal to the most universal.

In *hitbodedut*, a person relates directly to God in an intensely
natural and human way. He relates to God with the natural expression
that God gave him. Although he knows his soul is a part of God, he
knows that he must still open his mouth and create a personal dialogue
with God.

Hitbodedut addresses itself to all of a Jew's spiritual needs.

Sometimes a person has a goal in his conscious mind. *Hitbodedut*
can burn it into his subconscious so that he is now united in his effort
and desire to reach that goal.

Also, *hitbodedut* can clear up hidden conflicts and resolve previously unknown stumbling blocks to personal progress. It can help a
person make fine discriminations in dealing with a situation.

Source: *Likkutei Moharan* 2:25.

Still, Rabbi Nachman admonished us a great deal to pray the regular prayers.[2]

⋘

Hitbodedut and the Messiah

Rabbi Nachman said, "There are certainly kosher Jews who do not practice hitbodedut. But I call them confused.

"When the messiah suddenly comes and calls them, they will be confused.

"But we will be like a person waking up from a sleep with a calm mind. Our minds will be clear and undisturbed."[3]

⋘

Like Water on a Stone

Rabbi Nachman said that even if many years pass and it appears that one's hitbodedut has not accomplished anything, one should not be discouraged.

One's words actually are making an impression. Rabbi Nachman gave the analogy of water dropping on a stone. Even though it may appear that the water does not affect the stone, if the water keeps falling regularly, it will finally wear a hole through the stone.

Even if a person has a heart of stone and his prayer to God doesn't seem to be making any impression, over the course of many days and years, his words will wear a hole through it.[4]

⋘

The Spider Web

A certain person went to Rabbi Nachman several times and wanted to speak with him, but he couldn't open his mouth to tell Rabbi Nachman what was on his mind.

---

2. Source: *Likkutei Moharan* 2:97.
3. Source: *Sichot Haran*, no. 228.
4. Source: *Sichot Haran*, no. 234.

Once, when he was serving Rabbi Nachman, he decided to speak, but he couldn't even open his mouth.

When Rabbi Nachman came out of the bathhouse on a Friday afternoon, he told that man to hand him his shoes, so that he could put them on in honor of Shabbat. As the man handed the shoes to Rabbi Nachman, Rabbi Nachman told him, "Accustom yourself to speak before God. Then you will find it possible to speak with me."

Later, when this man had another chance to speak with Rabbi Nachman, he again found it difficult.

Rabbi Nachman said, "A soldier once attacked a stronghold. When he came to the gate, it was blocked by spider webs. Could there be a greater foolishness than turning back because of the spider webs?"

Afterward, Rabbi Nachman told this man that the essential thing is speech. Through speech, one can conquer everything and win all the wars. Although one can do *hitbodedut* in one's thoughts, the essential thing is to say the words out loud.

Sometimes it is difficult for a person to tell God or true *tzaddikim* what is in his heart. This is because he is embarrassed; he lacks the necessary holy brazenness. This is very foolish. The person wants to use his speech to conquer a great war—the war against his evil inclination. Now, when he is close to speaking, when he is close to conquering the wall and entering the gates, a small obstacle upsets him. Will he cease speaking? This obstacle is like a curtain of spider webs before the wall that he wishes to break with his speech.[5]

❦❦❦

Even One Word Is Very Good

Rabbi Nachman said that he made sure to engage in *hitbodedut* every day.

He said that even if one cannot speak, even if one can only say one word, that too is very good.

---

5. Source: *Sichot Haran*, no. 232.

If one can only say one word, one should repeat that word over and over. Even if one spends a few days on that one word, that too is good. One should keep repeating the word until God will have pity on him and open his mouth.[6]

⋘

The Power of Speech

Rabbi Nachman said that speech has great power. One can whisper to a rifle to keep it from shooting. Understand this.

Rabbi Nachman praised *hitbodedut* at great length. He encouraged us very much to engage in a great deal of *hitbodedut*.

He said that he wanted us to do *hitbodedut* every day and to spend the whole day on it.

But since not everyone can do this, a person should at least spend about an hour doing *hitbodedut*. This too is very good.

But if a person's heart is strong in serving God and he wants to truly take on the yoke of serving God, he should spend the whole day doing *hitbodedut*.

As our sages say, "Would that a person would pray the entire day" (*Berachot* 21).[7]

⋘

He Who Is Awake at Night

"Rabbi Chanina ben Chachinai said, 'He who is awake at night, goes on a path alone and turns his heart to void things—he makes his soul responsible'" (*Avot* 3:4).[8]

There are heretics who say that the world is a necessary

---

6. Source: *Likkutei Moharan* 2:96.

7. Source: *Likkutei Moharan* 2:96.

8. That is, he should have been studying Torah, but now, during a time that is susceptible to evil influences, he is engaged in empty matters.

existent. According to their evil and confused opinion, it appears
that they have proofs from the nature of the world.

But in truth, "their mouths have spoken vanity" (from Job
35:16). The world with everything in it is not a necessary
existent.

God alone is a necessary existent. All the universes with all
that is in them are not.

God created everything *ex nihilo*. It was within His ability to
either create them or not. Therefore, the entire universe with
everything in it is not a necessary existent.

But what is the source of the error that the world is a
necessary existent?

This comes from the fact that now, since the souls of Israel
have been emanated and drawn down, the world is on the level
of being a necessary existent.

The entire world and everything in it was only created for the
sake of Israel, as is known (*Leviticus Rabbah*, chap. 36, and
Rashi, beginning of Genesis).[9]

[In that sense,] Israel rules the world. Therefore, now, after

---

9. The recent doctrine of the strong anthropic principle states that
"the Universe (and hence the fundamental parameters on which it
depends) must be such as to admit the creation of observers within it at
some stage" (Brandon Carter of Cambridge, quoted in *The New Story
of Science*, by Robert M. Augros and George N. Stanciu [New York:
Bantam, 1984], p. 67). These observers are human beings. "[John]
Wheeler asserts that 'Quantum mechanics has led us to take seriously
and explore the . . . view that the observer is as essential to the
creation of the universe as the universe is to the creation of the
observer.' Though man is not at the physical center of the universe, he
appears to be at the center of its purpose" (ibid., p. 70).

The Talmud offers one definition of a member of Israel as one who
rejects idol worship.

If it is reasonable for scientists operating on a basis of scientific logic
to posit a universe that has man as its focal point, it is also reasonable
for a religious system to posit that our universe has as its focal point the
turning of man to God. There is one nation that has had, from the
earliest times, the doctrine of pure monotheism: the Jews. Thus, such
a system can reasonably say that the universe was created for the sake
of Israel.

the souls of Israel have been emanated and created, God was, so to speak, forced to create and maintain the world. He emanated the souls of Israel in order to create for them all the universes.

But at the point that they were emanated, the souls of Israel were themselves, with all the universes that depend on them, not a necessary existent, for it was within God's power to either emanate and create them or not. But as soon as God decided to emanate the souls of Israel, the whole world entered the level of being a necessary existent. This is because after the souls of Israel were emanated, God was obligated, so to speak, to make the world. Their souls were emanated so that all the universes would be created for them, and they would rule over everything. Understand this well.

From this has devolved the mistake of the heretics, who say that the world is a necessary existent.

But in truth, only God Himself is a necessary existent— nothing else.

The main reason that God created the universe for the sake of Israel was that the people of Israel will do His will and return and cleave to their root—that is, God, Who is the necessary existent. For this reason, He created everything.

Whenever the people of Israel do God's will and are absorbed in their root, which is the necessary existent, the entire universe that was created for their sake is absorbed into the necessary existent.

This is the purpose of the world's creation. It is only for the sake of Israel that God is obligated, so to speak, to create and maintain all the universes.

The more that Jews do God's will, the more are they absorbed with all the universes that depend on them into the necessary existent. Then all the worlds that depend on their souls are absorbed with them into the necessary existent.[10]

---

10. Although the world is somehow nullified before God and absorbed into Him, this is not a doctrine that teaches that this world is a meaningless illusion that must be shed before one can come to God.

In the teaching directly previous in *Likkutei Moharan*, Rabbi Nachman discusses how, after the coming of the messiah, the world

But this absorption into one's root—that is, in God's oneness,
Who is the necessary existent—is impossible unless one nullifies
oneself.

One must nullify oneself completely until one is absorbed into
God's oneness.

It is only possible to come to nullification via *hitbodedut.*

When one sets oneself aside and speaks freely to God, then
one can nullify all one's desires and bad character traits until
one nullifies all of one's physicality and is absorbed into one's
root.[11]

---

will revert to the high state of reality that existed before creation, when
everything will be one with God. This seems similar to the state
discussed here, when the entire world is nullified and absorbed into
God.

At the end of that teaching, Rabbi Nachman appends, "There is a
paradox about this that is impossible to understand. If it is so [that the
world will revert to a state of oneness], how is it that there will be a
difference in reward among different individuals, each receiving according to his level and according to the service and the effort he
expended in this world for the sake of God? At the ultimate end, people
won't be all equal. But since everything will be one, how can there be
a difference between individuals in regard to what level they are on?
This contains a secret that is impossible to understand, and these
matters are extremely deep."

In the present teaching as well, Rabbi Nachman is apparently
discussing a state where, in some paradoxical manner, the entire world
is absorbed into Godliness while at the same time retaining its sepa-
rateness and legitimate existence.

11. The phrase *nullifying oneself* is misleading. One is not nullifying one's self, but rather all those superficial characteristics that keep
one from being in touch with one's true, soul self.

In a similar vein, Rabbi Menachem Mendel Schneerson, the present
Lubavitcher rebbe, teaches that "one must serve God with self-
nullification, with the realization and awareness that all things that one
accomplishes with one's service, whether regarding oneself or another,
are not a result of one's own good points, but because one has been
given strength from on high. This awareness does not weaken one's
service. To the contrary, as a result of this awareness, one's service

Hitbodedut is in essence related to the night, when the world rests from its labors. During the day, when people are running after the things of this world, the world keeps a person from clinging to and being absorbed in God. Even if the person himself isn't taken up with this, since everyone else is running after the vanities of this world, it is hard for him to come to *bitul*.

Also, *hitbodedut* must be in a special place – that is, outside the city, in a lone, unfrequented area. A place that people frequent during the day, chasing after the things of this world, confuses one's *hitbodedut* even though they aren't there at present, and one cannot nullify oneself and be absorbed in God. One must go alone at night to a lone place, a place where there are no people. There one should do *hitbodedut*, turning one's heart and consciousness from all the things of this world, and nullifying everything until one comes to true *bitul*.

At first, one should engage in a great deal of prayer and talk in one's *hitbodedut* at night on a lone way, until one nullifies one unrefined character trait and lust. Then one should again engage a great deal in *hitbodedut* until one nullifies another such unrefined character trait. One should continue in this way for a

---

grows even stronger. When one's service is connected to one's situation, the service is limited and finite. This is true even when one is serving God 'with all your strength' (Deuteronomy 6:5) for one is limited to '*your* strength.' But when one realizes that the accomplishments of one's service are a result of the strengths one has because of the divine nature within one, then one transcends one's finite state of being, and one's service transcends limitations" (Rosh Hashanah talk of 5728 [1968], reprinted for Rosh Hashanah 5752 [1991]).

Bitul – nullification – is a nullification of this-worldly limitations that inhibit one's true self. When one accomplishes *bitul*, one does not become a mindless or passive agent. To the contrary, one becomes even more motivated and powerful than before.

Similarly, Rabbi Nachman points out that the power of *bitul* is not something that one uses to escape the universe, but rather to bring the entire universe to its ultimate state, which is total alignment with God's energy.

long time in *hitbodedut*, at that time and place, until one nullifies everything.

Afterward, when something is still left over, he should nullify that until nothing at all remains.

(That is to say, it is possible that even after he has nullified all of his lusts and bad traits, he still hasn't completely nullified his egotism and grossness, and he still appears to be a something in his own eyes. So he must toil and do a great deal of *hitbodedut* until nothing of him remains, until he truly reaches the spiritual level indicated by the word "what" and comes to the level of *bitul*.)

When he comes to true *bitul*, his soul is absorbed into its source – that is, into God, Who is the necessary existent. Then the entire world is absorbed with his soul into its source, which is the necessary existent, for everything depends on his soul. Then the whole world becomes a necessary existent.

Now you will see how all this is explained in the above-quoted *mishnah*.

"A person who is awake at night," in its simple meaning – he is awake at night and doing *hitbodedut*, speaking freely to God.

"And who goes on a lone road" – he goes on a lone path, in a place where people don't go. This is the best type of *hitbodedut*: at night on a lone path. Then one can come to the level of *bitul*.

"And turns one's heart to void things" – he turns his heart from all the things of this world to a void, in order to come to nullification.

Then one merits that one's soul will be absorbed into the necessary existent. Then all the universes are included with one's soul in the necessary existent.

"Behold, he is responsible for his soul." The entire world has been included with his soul into the necessary existence.[12]

Via *hitbodedut*, one reaches *bitul* when one's soul is absorbed into the necessary existent. As a result, the world has been absorbed together with one's soul into the necessary existent,

---

12. He literally "makes his soul responsible" (*mitchayev*), which is related to the word "necessary" (*mechuyav*).

and one's soul and all the world reach the level of being a necessary existent.[13]

❧❧❧

"I Will Run through the Marketplace!"

When Rabbi Nosson heard this teaching, he was so moved that his physical self was nullified and he cried out, "*Gevalt!* I will run through the marketplaces and streets and I will cry, *Gevalt!* What are people thinking about?"

His heart burned so strongly that he was practically no longer human. He really wanted to run out and shout like this.

But Rabbi Nachman grabbed him by his jacket and said to him, "Stay here. You won't accomplish anything."[14]

---

13. Source: *Likkutei Moharan* 1:52.
14. Source: *Kochavei Ohr*, p. 12.

23

The Power of Thought and Visualization

Speaking to the Body

Rabbi Nachman told one of his advanced, younger followers that during *hitbodedut*, he should speak a great deal in detail with all the limbs of his body, and explain to them that all the lusts of the body are vanity. The end of every man is death; the body will be brought to the grave, and all the limbs will wear away and decay; and so on.

The follower carried out this regimen for a period of time.

Afterward, he apologetically reported to Rabbi Nachman that his body wasn't responding to him at all.

Rabbi Nachman told him, "Be strong in this matter and do not slacken. You will eventually see results."

The follower listened to Rabbi Nachman's advice. Finally, he reached the state that whenever he spoke to one of his limbs in this way, its life force would literally leave it, and it would remain without strength or feeling.

This affected his senses in his outer limbs, such as his hands and feet, and it also began to affect his inner organs, such as his heart. He was forced to limit his words so that his lifeforce wouldn't leave him entirely.

I heard that once this man was talking to some friends about how this world is nothing, what eventually happens to the body, and so on, and in the midst of his words, he fainted away, and great efforts were needed to revive him.

After he came to, he said that he had come to such a level via the holiness of Rabbi Nachman. Now, every time he reminded himself of the fear of punishment in the world-to-come and the end of all the things of this world, all his limbs, even his small toe, would feel as though they were already lying in the grave and decaying, until he would need a great deal of strength to keep his soul from leaving his body.[1]

❮❮❮

Thought and Visualization

Thought has great power. A person can achieve anything that he strengthens and intensifies his thought about. For instance, if he concentrates his thought on having money, he will certainly become wealthy. The same holds true regarding any other matter.

This thought must be accompanied by the nullification of all feelings [i.e., sensory impressions]. The thought must be so powerful that one could sacrifice himself with it. That is, one could consciously decide that one is prepared to die for the sake of sanctifying God's name and actually feel the pain of that death. It is possible to so intensify one's thought that at the time that one visualizes that one is ready to die for the sake of sanctifying God's name, one will literally feel the pain of death.

[At the time of his death by torture,] Rabbi Akiva said, "All my life I worried over this verse [of Sh'ma,] thinking, when will I be able to fulfill it? And now I can" (Berachot 61b).

During the reading of the Sh'ma, Rabbi Akiva used to visualize the four death penalties imposed by a Jewish court. He accepted

---

1. Source: Chayei Moharan 2:46, no. 6.

death with such a powerful thought that he literally felt the suffering of death, as though he were actually being executed.

This is what is meant: "All my days I worried – literally, suffered – when will I be able to fulfill and sacrifice myself for the sake of the sanctification of God's name? From this thought alone, I would suffer the pain of death. Now that it is actually occurring, shall I not fulfill it? After all, I was already suffering this when I accepted it mentally."

When a person strengthens his thought to this degree, he can literally die from this pain, as though he were dying from that actual death. There is no difference between the actual death and the pain that he feels from the imagined death.

A person must hold himself back from remaining in that state, so that he will not die before his time, God forbid.[2]

---

2. One can of course adapt this technique to a visualization that feels comfortable for oneself. For instance, one could visualize that all of one's limbs are being infused with spiritual light.

Source: *Likkutei Moharan* 1:193.

24

Women in Rabbi Nachman's Life

Honoring One's Wife

Rabbi Nachman admonished us to honor our wives. He said, "Women suffer a great deal from pregnancy, childbirth, and bringing up children. Everyone knows how many difficult experiences they have. A person should respect his wife and treat her with a great deal of love. Besides, our sages said, 'Honor your wives in order that you become wealthy' (*Bava Metzia* 59a), and 'It is enough for us that they raise our children [and keep us from sin (i.e., sinful thoughts – Rashi)]' (*Yevamot 63a*)."[1]

❮❮❮

Feiga – Rabbi Nachman's Mother

At the beginning of *Elul*, [5560], Rabbi Nachman married off his daughter, Adil. The wedding was in Chmelnik, and Rabbi Nachman attended the wedding with his entire family, as is

---

1. Source: *Sichot Haran*, no. 264.

customary. His mother, the saintly Feiga, also attended the wedding. She saw the departed Baal Shem Tov present at the wedding canopy, for she was a saintly woman who had an inspired spirit. All the *tzaddikim* said that she possessed an inspired spirit and that she was on a very high level. In particular, her brothers, the well-known *tzaddikim* – i.e., the holy Rabbi [Ephraim] of Sudylkov [author of *Degel Machaneh Ephraim*] and the holy Rabbi Boruch [of Medziboz] – held that she was a prophetess.[2]

⋘

Sashia – Rabbi Nachman's First Wife

Once, the Baal Shem Tov said, "If my first wife were still alive, I would ascend to heaven in the middle of the day in public, in the marketplace of Medziboz; not like Elijah, who went up to heaven in the desert."

And once Rabbi Nachman said, "If I had known the great worth of a first marriage, I would have told my wife, 'Be sick, but at least stay alive' " (for his first wife was sick for a long time).[3]

⋘

Rabbi Nachman's Daughters

Rabbi Nachman said, "My children [editor's note: i.e., his daughters] have holy inspiration, which is close to prophecy; and I am not even talking about my daughter, Sarah."[4]

⋘

A Letter to Sarah

Rabbi Nachman once sent a letter to his daughter, Sarah, filled with great love and affection, in which he wrote that he yearned

---

2. Source: *Chayei Moharan* 1:54, no. 11.
3. Source: *Avanehah Barzel*, p. 39.
4. Source: *Chayei Moharan* 2:69, no. 131.

for her to be with him so that he could constantly delight in her and receive wisdom and awe of heaven from her words.

He wrote, "Now, you are like a myrtle in the desert, where no one can appreciate its scent."[5]

☙☙☙

Receiving Praise

When Sarah received this letter, she read it in the presence of several Bratslaver *Chasidim*. She broke into tears, and told them, "If my father praises me like this, I must be on a very low level. I once heard my father say to Rabbi Nosson that at times he praises someone to his face because he sees that the person fell from his level and he needs to encourage him."[6]

☙☙☙

Rabbi Nachman's Second Wife

Rabbi Nachman's second wife said of him, "I imagine you, I call you, but I have not known you" (quoting *Shir Hakavod*, a twelfth-century liturgical poem attributed to Rabbi Yehudah Hahasid Regensburg).[7]

---

5. Source: *Chayei Moharan* 2:69, no. 129.
6. Source: *Chayei Moharan* 2:69, no. 130.
7. Source: Aryeh Kaplan, *Until the Mashiach—The Life of Rabbi Nachman: An Annotated Chronology*, ed. Dovid Shapiro (Jerusalem: The Breslov Research Institute, 1985), p. 144.

25

Marriage

Knowledge Causes Marriages

Knowledge causes marriages.[1]

All marriages are of two opposites; knowledge is the go-between between these two opposites.[2]

Therefore, all marriages are brought about by the master of knowledge.[3]

---

1. The word for knowledge, *daat*, signifies the joining together of man and woman, as in the verse, "Adam knew Eve, his wife." It also implies the joining together of opposites, for the spiritual force of *daat* joins together the opposite male and female forces of wisdom and understanding.

2. See *Likkutei Moharan* 1:4.

3. Here we go beyond the realm of Torah psychology to the realm of one's connection to a master of Torah.

Just as Rabbi Nachman says that a person should only pray with the mystical intentions of the *Ari* when they are a natural part of him, so one may say that one is only able to look for a *tzaddik* when this is a natural, organic process in the context of a developed, healthy self.

But it is easy to use such teachings by Rabbi Nachman as this one to

At times it is hard for a person to find his spouse, for the two people are distant from each other. They are extreme opposites.

The rectification for this is to come to the master of knowledge and hear Torah from his lips. One can then find one's spouse. As long as knowledge is *in potentia*, it can be impossible to bring together the two people if they are greatly opposed to each other, for sometimes these two people are extremely different from one another. Then, as long as the knowledge is in potentia, it cannot bring them together.

One must hear the Torah from this man's mouth. The knowledge then emerges, on the level of "from his mouth comes knowledge and understanding" (Proverbs 2:6). When the knowledge goes from potentiality to actuality, these two people can marry, even if they are very much opposite to each other.

This is why the acronym of *shidduch*, marriage, is "the lips of a cohen will guard knowledge and Torah" (Malachi 2:7).

"They will seek it from his lips" (Malachi 2:7). One must seek the Torah from his lips in order to bring the knowledge from potential to actuality.

Even though there is also knowledge in the simple words of the master of knowledge, one must specifically hear Torah from his lips.

This is because the Torah is called a bride, as in the saying of the sages, "Do not read 'an inheritance,' but rather 'a fiancee' " (referring to the verse, "Moses gave us the Torah, an inheritance" [Deuteronomy 33]—i.e., the Torah is "the bride of all Israel" [Rashi] [*Pesachim* 49b]).

The Torah itself contains opposites, for it has two types of letters.[4]

When the *tzaddik* speaks words of Torah, this is the level of making marriages. The words of Torah are sparse in one spot

---

escape a difficult reality. If a person is having difficulty getting married, he may approach this teaching as a magic formula, hoping that as a result of mechanically seeking a spiritual master, he will find his spouse, rather than doing the hard work of dealing with the reality of his environment and of his own psyche.

4. See introduction to the *Zohar*, "large letters and small letters."

and expansive in another (Jer. *Rosh Hashanah*, chap. *Ra'uhu Beit Din*). One gathers words of Torah from scattered places, which are distant from each other, and joins them together.

Then one creates novel Torah thoughts.

In sum, when the *tzaddik*, the master of knowledge, says words of Torah, he causes marriages. Therefore, one must listen to words of Torah from his mouth.

As a result, one can find one's spouse.[5]

⋙

The Many Levels of True Marriage

Rabbi Nachman said that when he went in Radvill to get engaged to his second wife from Brody, several women came seeking to get engaged to him.

He said that each one of them was his marriage partner.

He said that every person has a number of partners. However, various levels and extraordinary matters are involved.

When words are spoken regarding a possible marriage, even if they aren't brought to completion, that itself is a level of marriage.

---

5. The only true reality is Torah; everything else is a reflection of that. Whatever one accomplishes on the realm of Torah automatically affects analogous processes in the world. When one causes the process of marriage in the letters of the Torah, one automatically brings out the analogous process of marriage between a man and a woman. It is not that marriage between a man and a woman is the true reality and the marriage of Torah concepts a metaphor for marriage, but the contrary: the archetype of marriage is within the letters and spiritual energies of Torah, and it is reflected in human reality, as marriage.

Since the only person on the level of this reality is the *tzaddik*, one must go to him and hear him speak words of Torah and create a marriage within words of Torah. Then one is witness and partner to the spiritual energy flow of marriage, and this affects one's own life and consciousness. Then, one's spiritual "force field" is properly aligned, and one is able to find one's spouse.

Source: *Likkutei Moharan* 2:89.

Sometimes, people say that so-and-so should marry so-and-so. This itself completes the level of a marriage of those two people.

Sometimes, matchmakers discuss a match, but it isn't completed. This too is a match, more than the first instance.

Sometimes, people travel to make a match, and when it is being finalized, for some reason it falls apart.

And sometimes the match is completed but afterward the engagement is broken off.

And sometimes the couple gets married and soon afterward divorces.

And sometimes they are only divorced after a long time.

And there are many other incomplete levels of marriage.

But in all of these cases, one has been linked to one's true partner.

This is because every person has a number of partners.

The difference between them is that with one, the match is concluded by a word; with another through more words; with another, through some travel or action for the sake of the marriage; and so on.

A simple conversation regarding a marriage is itself on the level of a marriage.

It is clear that Rabbi Nachman knew awesome secrets regarding this that weren't revealed to the world, as was his way in all his awesome insights.

People say that Rabbi Nachman boasted then that he knows things regarding marriages regarding which all the leaders of the generation know nothing.[6]

⋘

Marital Harmony

Once, on either Shavuot or Hannukah, as Rabbi Nachman sat at the table with his followers, he said, "Who has the temerity to have a sexual thought at my table?"

---

6. Source: *Chayei Moharan* 2:73, no. 143.

He continued, "I don't mean the Tcheriner, nor the Bratslaver, nor the Tepliker."

But he didn't mention the man from Tirovich, who had not had good relations with his wife for two years.

Immediately, Rabbi Nachman got up from the table and went into his room.

This man went to Rabbi Nachman's door and cried a great deal, and Rabbi Nachman's followers also beseeched Rabbi Nachman on his behalf.

The man promised that he would immediately make peace with his family.[7]

◄◄◄

The Groom from the World-to-Come

Rabbi Nachman told that he dreamed that he went to a wedding.

I knew the name of the groom.

I looked around and saw a person from the world-to-come, a dead man. I was very surprised and said to myself, "If the other people see him, there will be a great commotion." I knew the name of this dead person.

The names of the groom and the dead person weren't earthly names, but spiritual names that hint at certain matters, like other holy names.

Afterward, the other people also saw this dead person.

I said to them, "Isn't this person dead?'

They only replied, "Still and all," and they weren't disturbed.

Afterward, I decided to go to the synagogue, from which I would have a better view of the wedding. I circled around like this (Rabbi Nachman showed with his finger how he circled around) and I came to the synagogue. At the wedding canopy, the people sang to the groom, "You are a young man, you are a groom." I knew the tune. It was a lovely melody, a melody of joy.

I looked at the scene from the synagogue. Then I decided that I didn't like that location either, and I went to my house. When

---

7. Source: *Avanehah Barzel*, p. 28.

I came to my house, I found the groom there, lying on the
ground. I woke him up: "Aren't they singing to you so much
[over there], yet you are lying here?"

(Afterward, Rabbi Nachman said himself that it was an extraordinary thing that they were singing to him so much over
there, while he was lying down here. And the matter is hidden
and concealed.)

Rabbi Nachman said that in the dream it appeared to him that
the place of the synagogue has a different name and the place
where he went to his house has a different name. (He said that he
knew it but forgot it. I am not sure whether he was referring to
the tune or the names of the places. But he said that he still
knows the names of the groom and the dead person.)

He added that there are other things in this dream that he
saw.[8]

---

8. Source: *Chayei Moharan* 1:43, no. 13.

26

Sexuality

There Really Is No Lust at All

There is really no lust at all. Eating and drinking are necessary to maintain the body. One must also have children. A person must do all these things. And so there is no lust at all. There is only one condition: one must act in holiness and purity.[1]

❧❧❧

---

1. Rabbi Hatzadok, an eighteenth-century student of Bratslav *Chasidim* and himself a great teacher, writes in a similar vein, "All natural entities do the will of God. When a person engages in natural activities that his nature forces him to engage in, this is called 'doing the will of one's Creator,' and an element of *mitzvah* is involved in the matter. Eating, drinking, and sexual relations are in [a man's] nature, just as they are in the nature of creatures who lack free will, as long as they are done out of necessity"—*Tzidkat Hatzaddik*, no. 173.

Source: *Sichot Haran*, no. 51.

One Can Withstand All Lusts

A person's consciousness can withstand all lusts.

"The Holy One, blessed be He, gives wisdom to the wise" (Daniel 2:21).

Everyone has wisdom in potential. But it must be brought into actuality.

With no more than the wisdom that everyone has in potential, besides that wisdom that is given to the wise, one can withstand lusts.

Even if a person is drawn after the lusts of this world and has engaged in transgressions that have polluted and constricted his mind, his remaining clear consciousness can still rise up. Even one point of consciousness can withstand the entire world with all its lusts.

Wherever one is, one can be close to God.

Even in the depths of hell, one can come close to God and truly serve Him.

One needs either mercy from God or hard work, if not both together, before one reaches the point that the dregs of one's lower mind are quieted and one wants nothing of this world.

When one achieves this, everything will be equal in one's eyes (Proverbs 6:22). "When you go, it will guide you, when you lie down, it will guard you, and when you awake, it will communicate with you" (Proverbs 6:22).

One will experience no difference between this world, the grave, and the world-to-come.

" 'When you go, it will guide you' – the Torah will guide you in this world. 'When you lie down, it will guard you' – when you lie in the grave, God and the Torah are there with you. 'And when you awake' – to the world to come – 'it will communicate with you' " (based on *Avot*, 6:9).

When a person is connected to this world, there is a separation between this world, which is so broad, and the grave, which is so narrow. But when a person's mind has been purified and his mind no longer contains dregs, everything is equal in his eyes.

Since such a person has no desire for anything but God and

Torah, everything else is equal in his eyes—whether in this world, the grave, or the world-to-come. In all these states, he just clings to God and to the Torah.[2]

≪≪≪

Abstinence

Our sages said, "If a young Torah scholar sits and fasts, thus growing weak, a dog should eat his food" (*Taanit* 11b).

The eating of a *tsaddik* is very precious, for with it he satisfies his holy soul. As the verse says, "A *tsaddik* eats to satisfy his soul" (Proverbs 13:25).

But since this young Torah scholar starved his soul and doesn't know how to feed it, "a dog should eat his food." We learn that dogs "do not know satisfaction" (Isaiah 56:11). This person also does not know how to satisfy his precious soul.

A dog is called *shegel* (*Rosh Hashanah* 4a), for the dog has a strong sexual desire [*mishgal*].

This only refers to a case where a person fasts even though he does not have to. However, if a person has to fast, he should, and it is a *mitzvah* to do so (*Bach* on *Orach Chayyim* 571). That is why our sages said, "who *sits* and fasts"—i.e., he sits in one place spiritually and does not change.[3]

---

2. Source: *Sichot Haran*, no. 51.

3. The eating and fasting referred to here hint at sexual activity. (Eating is a common euphemism for sexuality.) A person may want to refrain from sexuality in order to be more spiritual. But since this is premature, not only does he not use his spiritual energy well (he doesn't feed his soul) but he misuses and misdirects his sexual energy (a dog should eat his food). Such restraint doesn't indicate any change or growth in his spiritual status.

However, if a person is a *tsaddik* and finds that he must refrain, as did Moses, it is a *mitzvah* to do so.

Source: *Likkutei Moharan* 1:50.

₭₭₭

Equal in His Eyes

Rabbi Nachman said that man and woman were equal before
him – he didn't have the slightest sexual thought when he saw a
woman.

He once said that he is afraid of neither woman nor angel.
There is much to explain regarding this.

If a person has even the slightest fear of having sexual
thoughts, even if he only has a slight bit of fear, he must fear the
angel.

But Rabbi Nachman boasted that he had no fear of this, and so
he was not afraid of the angel.[4]

₭₭₭

Who Is Forcing You?

Once, Rabbi Nachman spoke about the lust for sexual unseemliness. He ridiculed this lust a great deal.

He said, "I always find it difficult to understand why our sages
said that when having physical relations, one should imagine
that one is being forced by a demon. Who is forcing you?"

If a person wants to conquer his desire completely, no one can
force him. Understand this.[5]

---

4. Source: *Sichot Haran* 1:18.

5. "Sexual unseemliness" refers to a desire that overtakes one's
sense of propriety and of being in the sight of God.

Rabbi Nachman was on a level where his involvement in sexuality
was entirely voluntary; he didn't experience any compulsion that
disturbed him in the entirety of his life.

The Talmud states that, according to one opinion, a man should
engage in sexual relations "as though a demon is pushing him." This is
not to state that the act itself is demonic. This act serves as the prime
metaphor for the relations between God and Israel, as in the Song of
Songs and kabbalistic texts. Precisely because this act is so fraught with
holiness and powerful spiritual energy, it attracts negative spiritual

€€€

A Platonic Marriage

Rabbi Nachman married his second wife on condition that they would not live together as man and wife.[6]

€€€

The Harm of Lust

Once, Rabbi Nachman spoke of removing oneself from the lust for sexual immorality.

He said that when one eats, the food at least gives one strength and life.

But as regards this lust, the opposite is true. It reduces and harms a person's life force and is very harmful.

If not for the need to perpetuate the species, it would not be necessary at all.[7]

---

forces that come to feed from it and that can drag a person down into a realm of subservience to his physical pleasure, divorced from a sense of identification with his spirituality. When a person has physical relations, it should be "as though a demon is pushing him"–with the consciousness that he is susceptible to becoming subservient to his purely physical senses and to losing touch with Godliness.

Source: *Chayei Moharan* 2:62, no. 84.

6. At this point, Rabbi Nachman also exhibited the first signs of tuberculosis, from which he was to die three years later.

Source: *Until the Mashiach*, p. 144.

7. Some sexuality is engaged in solely for physical pleasure, in a manner that removes one from a connection to spirituality and from human self-respect. Such a lust is harmful and reduces a person's life force.

Although there have been many dynamic people who have had sordid private lives (see Paul Johnson's *Intellectuals* [New York: Harper and Row, 1988]), those people's link to spirituality and quite often to basic human decency has been severely attenuated.

Source: *Likkutei Moharan* 2:107.

⋘

A Test That Is Not a Test

The extremely great level of Rabbi Nachman's holiness in conquering his sexual lust cannot be explicated.

He said that he had had endless tests – but that this is really no test at all, because it is not lust at all.

He said that if a person is simply wise, whether Jewish or not, he shouldn't consider this a desire at all.[8]

Rabbi Nachman said that if a person knows human anatomy, he should find this desire totally uninteresting. He spoke a great deal regarding the primitive nature of this lust.[9]

In general, Rabbi Nachman treated this lust with the greatest contempt and disdain. He once even stated that a person who is even a little bit wise won't view this desire as a test at all.

But before Rabbi Nachman reached the level of nullifying this and being able to treat it with the utmost disdain, he had many great and terrible tests.

When Rabbi Nachman was young and his blood was hot, he had numberless tests. It was within his power to fulfill his lust

---

8. Within the context of Judaism, a man is obligated to be married. This is a context within which "lust" is not identical with normal relations, but additional to them. As Maimonides states, celibacy can lead to physical illness (*Hilchot Dei'ot* 4:19).

Rabbi Nachman was speaking in an era in which sexuality was a much more muted part of life than it is today. Today, lewdness has become part of the daily background of most people's lives – it is one of the principal tools of the commercial society we live in. A basic and natural part of the human being is being artificially aroused many times per day. A person today is more likely to find himself prey to sexual thoughts than he might have in the milieu of Rabbi Nachman.

9. After a person has taken care of his basic needs, any remaining desires are based solely on his imagination. If he were to view in a totally cold manner the pure physicality of what he is finding sexually fascinating, he would not continue to be erotically interested.

and he was in very great danger. But he was very strong and he overcame his desire many times.[10]

Rabbi Nachman said that the Satan wanted to allow him everything as long as he would give in on this. But Rabbi Nachman said that to the contrary, he would set aside everything else but not this.

This is how he acted from the beginning, for his entire purpose was to first break this lust.[11]

Rabbi Nachman said that this is no lust at all. He spoke of this a great deal, regarding the emptiness and degraded nature of this lust.

He said that it is impossible to speak of this matter with people who are immersed in physicality. Their blood is so turbid that their consciousness is confused, and so they cannot understand that it is possible to have disdain for this.

Therefore, it is impossible to speak much of this.

But if a person is even a little wise, he can easily treat this desire with complete disdain.

Rabbi Nachman said that to a person who is even slightly wise, this is no test at all.

He said that there must be a secret in this matter, for it is no desire at all.

He lavishly praised his achievement in overcoming this lust. He was extraordinarily holy regarding this matter. He said that he has no lust whatsoever.[12]

---

10. Rabbi Nachman was married when he was 13 or 14 years old. *Until the Mashiach* (by Rabbi Aryeh Kaplan and edited by Rabbi Dovid Shapiro; Jerusalem, Breslov Research Institute, 1985) states that Rabbi Nachman's sexual tests occurred after his marriage.

11. As Rabbi Nosson goes on to explain, this practice was within the context of an ascetic way of life that would be extreme for any but the most accomplished spiritual personality – and even for such a personality, it may be that the atmosphere and era for such self-mortification no longer exists. Although self-mortification is often an obsessive drive used by people who have psychological problems, it can be a conscious and effective tool in the interests of spiritual growth by those who have mastery over themselves.

12. Source: *Sichot Haran* 1:17.

❧❧❧

By Me, It Is Absolutely Nothing

Rabbi Nachman said, "If our sages hadn't explicitly stated that it is forbidden to verbally challenge evil spiritual forces by stating 'an arrow in the eye of Satan,' I would say it.

"I can't understand the stories in the Talmud about some of our sages who found lust to be so troublesome.

"By me, it is nothing, absolutely nothing.

"I don't consider this a test at all. There is certainly a secret in the Torah's statement that this lust is a test, because it is really no test at all.

"If a person knows a bit of the greatness of the Creator, he does not consider this as any kind of test.

"I see no difference between a man and a woman. I see this lust the same way I see you.[13] I have had endless tests. But this is not a test at all." (But in his youth, he too had a number of tests.)[14]

The evil inclination exists on various levels.

Some people are very low and corporeal. Their evil inclination is also low and corporeal.

---

13. Rabbi Nachman no longer experienced this lust as part of himself but as something removed from himself; thus, he viewed it the way he would view anything outside of himself.

14. *Chayei Moharan* 2:5, no. 4.

The Talmud tells of tests regarding sexual temptation that befell a number of *tzaddikim*. Such stories teach that, in the words of the Talmud, "the greater the *tzaddik*, the greater is his desire."

The greater a person is, the greater is his connection to his eros, his life force. Since sexuality is intimately connected to life force, both personal and universal, when a person becomes a *tzaddik*, his channel of erotic energy grows as well. This is not to say that he becomes a lustful person, but rather that the channel through which sexuality passes is also a channel for eros.

A *tzaddik* doesn't suppress his sexual being, but transforms it and uses it. Since this energy is still in force, it can at times revert to basic sexual desire, in a context where the fulfillment of that desire would be a sin. Thus, the Talmud tells of sages who had to battle an impulse to sexually misbehave.

The evil inclination of most people is the blood in the left hollow of the heart, in its full strength.

These people are confused by the turbidity and confusion of their blood.

When a person attains a measure of clear consciousness, he regards this evil inclination as great foolishness and madness, and he doesn't need any special strength to conquer it.

He even regards something that most people would regard as a great test, such as sexual impropriety, as foolishness. He doesn't see it as a any kind of test.

When a person has a somewhat clear measure of consciousness and knows a little of the greatness of God, when he achieves the level of imagining the greatness of God, he does not regard anything as a test, and needs no special strength to overcome this.

However, there is an evil inclination that is a holy angel. One needs to overcome this as well.

This is the level of severities, the level of judgments.

The spiritually conscious master has this evil inclination of severities and judgments. He must overcome it and sweeten the judgments, so that everything will become completely good.

When a person is absorbed into the Infinite One, everything is good, and there is no judgment.

One must be completely good; one must sweeten all severities and judgments, which are the supernal evil inclination.

It is on this level that David erred with Bathsheba.

God forbid that one should say that David physically sinned because of a desire. David himself said, "My heart is hollow within me" (Psalms 109:23), meaning that he had already killed

---

Rabbi Nachman might be saying that the spiritual dynamics of his era had changed and that it was now possible to reach a level of spiritual virility not subject to physical temptation.

One would then have to deal with the stories in the Bible that tell of great *tzaddikim* who were subject to sexual temptation. Whereas it is audacious for a rabbi to declare himself to be in some ways on a higher level than the sages of the Talmud, it is unthinkable for him to do so regarding the figures of the Bible.

Rabbi Nachman now addresses himself to this issue.

his physical evil inclination and subjugated the blood in the left hollow of his heart.

Our sages said, "Whoever says that David sinned is mistaken" (*Shabbat* 56a). Even the small flaw that occurred was not due to a desire that came from the turbidity of the blood, from which comes the lust for sexual impropriety.

Rather, David's flaw came from a supernal source in severities. He hadn't sweetened his evil inclination on the supernal realm — that is, on the level of severities and judgments.

This was very subtle, for our sages teach that "Bathsheba was fit for David" (*Sanhedrin* 107a).

The verse says of David, "You shall not build a house for My name, for you have spilled much blood" (1 Chronicles 22:8) — that is, he didn't sweeten the severities, [which are referred to as blood]. Therefore, he did not merit to build the Temple.

Even though David fought the war of God, nevertheless, on the highest supernal level (which is the place where he should have been absorbed, the level of the Infinite One, where everything is entirely good), things must be enirely good, meaning, without any severities at all. . . .

One should also not imagine that when King Solomon married the daughter of Pharaoh and many other Gentile women, this came from a physical evil inclination. He was a true wise man, as the verse says, "He was more wise than any man" (1 Kings 5:11).

Whoever is even a little wise doesn't consider this lust to be any sort of temptation. Even if a beautiful woman were to proposition him in a secluded place and he could fulfill this lust, he would regard it as foolishness and madness, and he would not see it as any kind of a test.

As for the Torah's praise of Joseph's withstanding [Potiphar's wife], a mystical secret is involved.

Again, their test was on the level of sweetening the severities and conquering the supernal evil inclination, not conquering the physical evil inclination, for that is no test at all.[15]

---

15. But if "we have a principle that whoever is even a little bit wise doesn't consider this lust to be a temptation at all," how can it be that

€€€

The Litmus Test

Someone praised a well-known *tzaddik* to Rabbi Nachman, and said that he had broken his desires for food and drink.

Rabbi Nachman asked, "But what about sexual desire?"

The man replied, "Who can tell?"

Rabbi Nachman answered, "This desire is the essential thing. It is easy to break other desires. But a person is considered a *tzaddik* only if he manages to break this desire entirely."[16]

---

the sages of the Talmud, who were certainly a lot more than "even a little bit wise," did consider this lust to be an active temptation?

Just as Rabbi Nachman spiritually interprets the temptations of the figures of the Bible, so might he interpret the stories of the sages of the Talmud.

The sages say that one should not challenge the evil inclination by saying "an arrow in the eye of Satan." This is a general admonition to the general populace. Rabbi Nachman—or a true *tzaddik* in general—is on a level where he can challenge the evil inclination. However, because the sages of the Talmud have forbidden it as a general principle, he is constrained to avoid doing so. Perhaps this is a way of saying that there are certain spiritual rectifications that Rabbi Nachman could accomplish, symbolized by the phrase, "An arrow in the eye of Satan," but which the spiritual framework laid down by the sages made it impossible for him to do. Therefore, such accomplishments, which would have brought the messianic age closer, must proceed on a more gradual manner and in other ways.

Source: *Likkutei Moharan* 1:72.

16. Source: *Chayei Moharan* 2:74, no. 149.

Rabbi Nachman teaches as though nature and natural needs do not exist. However, for all except the greatest *tzaddikim*, such needs do exist. He teaches of sexuality in an ideal, extreme manner that posits a *tzaddik* who is only involved in service of God and no longer concerned with his nature.

Rabbi Nachman seems to say that one serves God through nullifying one's physicality, in particular, one's sexuality.

Yet eros is the root of one's life energy. In suppressing one's sexual

€€€

Marital Relations and Shabbat

The most important time of one's relationships with one's wife is on Friday night, Shabbat eve. At that time, one is absorbed into holiness, and all "workers of iniquity" are removed.[17]

Then, Deuteronomy states, "You will eat and be satisfied" (Deuteronomy 8:10). This is a reference to Shabbat, which is the time of being satisfied, for it is from the Shabbat that the six days of the week are blessed (*Zohar*).[18]

---

energy, one necessarily suppresses and twists all of one's energies, including the spiritual.

When a person identifies with his animal soul, he must express his sexual energy as the root of his spiritual energy.

But when a person identifies with his Godly soul, he doesn't identify with his sexual energy. In such a case, the teachings of Rabbi Nachman apply.

The animal soul is very extensive and includes feelings of spirituality and closeness to God. Almost all people operate on the level of the animal soul.

In addition, Rabbi Nachman's description of sexuality as something to be disdained may be apropos only for a state of consciousness in which integration between body and spirituality is not really possible. Such a generation may be on a high spiritual level, but unable to deal with its eros. However, our present generation, although much smaller than Rabbi Nachman's generation in many ways, is possibly more open to the concepts and possibilities of leading an integrated life. This new burden and responsibility of integration itself contributes to a lowered spiritual level. Nowadays, one's spirituality cannot be nurtured by itself, but one must accomplish the much more difficult job of nurturing and attempting to integrate various aspects of oneself that are often at basic odds: e.g., one's physicality, one's emotional needs, and one's spirituality.

17. In the proper spirit, sexuality is a holy act. In line with Jewish law, Shabbat is precisely the most central time for such relations to take place.

18. Source: *Likkutei Moharan* 1:39.

‹‹‹

Marriage and Circumcision

Rabbi Nachman said that the true *tzaddik* finds marital relations to be very difficult. Not only does he experience no lust, but he suffers like a baby being circumcised.

The *tzaddik* suffers even more than a baby. A baby has no consciousness, but since the *tzaddik* is conscious, his sufferings are greater.

This was a simple thing for Rabbi Nachman. He said that anyone could achieve such a level.

It appears from his words that his own level of holiness was much higher than this.[19]

‹‹‹

Rectifying a Nonmarital Emission

One rectifies a nocturnal emission by reciting ten chapters of psalms on the day of the occurrence. . . .

One must say ten chapters, for there are ten types of song, which are the ten categories of psalms (*Pesachim* 117, and

---

19. A person can come to a level of self-control where he does not identify with his body and thus he does not identify with his bodily desires.

Circumcision is an act of purification and perfection of sexuality. When a person separates himself from his physical desires, he again experiences an act of holiness and sexual purification. The *tzaddik* feels with full consciousness the pain that necessarily accompanies such a sexual purification.

Most people do not experience this. Nevertheless, whether for a *tzaddik* or an ordinary human being, the marital act is essentially one of sexual holiness reminiscent of the act of circumcision.

Source: *Shivchei Haran*, no. 17.

Zohar)–"Fortunate is the man; To the choir leader; A Teaching Psalm; Hallelu-yah," and so on.

Each category has the power to nullify the power of the shell [of uncleanness], for each one of these languages is the opposite of the shell. . . .

After this teaching, Rabbi Nachman revealed the ten psalms that one should say: 16, 32, 41, 42, 59, 77, 90, 105, 137, 150. He said that they comprise a very great rectification for an emission. A person who says them the same day does not have to worry about the terrible flaw caused by a nocturnal emission, for it has certainly been rectified.[20]

❀❀❀

The Messiah and Sexual Sin

Through the merit of the rectification of this sexual sin, the messiah will come to gather the scattered Jews.[21]

❀❀❀

The Power of Ten Psalms

Rabbi Nachman said that one must be careful to go to the mikveh the same day that one has a nocturnal emission.

Some people have such an occurrence because they ate or drank a great deal, or because of weakness and tiredness, or because they lay on their stomachs. Such occurrences are meaningless, like a child who wets his bed.

But when a person has an emission as a result of having engaged in sexual fantasies, this creates an evil influence.

However, when one recites these ten chapters of psalms on the same day, he causes a tremendous rectification.

If a person goes to the mikveh and then says the ten psalms,

---

20. Source: Likkutei Moharan 1:205.
21. Source: Likkutei Moharan 2:92.

that is very good. But even if he can't go to the *mikveh*, it is still very good.

If a person says the psalms with the proper intent, it is very good. But even just reciting the words is good.

This rectification has not been known since the creation of the world.

"You can imagine that I would have wanted to nullify this entirely.

"But it is impossible, both physically and spiritually.

"Physically, it is impossible, for it would mean permanently changing the nature of mankind. Even Moses could only nullify nature, for a limited period and regarding a specific event, such as the splitting of the Red Sea.

"In spirituality it is also impossible."

Rabbi Nachman said that even after he dies, when someone will come to his grave, recite these ten psalms and give a coin to charity, even if he has committed a great many sins, "I will do everything I can to save him and rectify him. I am very sure about everything that I do and say. But I am especially sure that these ten psalms help a great deal."

One should say the ten psalms in order.

They comprise a general rectification. Every sin has its particular rectification. But this rectification is general.

This should be taught to everyone.

Even though it is an easy thing to say ten chapters of psalms, it will be very hard to carry out.[22]

᭣᭣᭣

Rectifying Self-Arousal

The *Zohar* states (Genesis 188a, 219b) that repentance does not help a person who sexually misbehaved, in particular one who masturbated.

Rabbi Nachman said that this is not so. Repentance helps for everything.

---

22. Source: *Sichot Haran*, no. 141.

He said that only he understands the meaning of this passage from the *Zohar*.

Even if one engaged in this sin a great deal, repentance really helps.

Many books have already been printed, explaining that one proves that one has repented when, finding oneself in identical circumstances as before, one resists engaging in the sin.[23]

❮❮❮

The Arrows and the Castle of Water

On the sixth day, the newlywed couple was again joyful, and longed for the beggar without hands.

The beggar entered and said, "Here I am. I came to your wedding" – and he continued, telling them what the other beggar had said. Then he embraced and kissed them. And he told them:

"You think that I am crippled in my hands. This is not so. I have strength in my hands, but I do not use the power of my hands in this world, because I need that power for something else. And I have a testimony to this effect from the castle of water.

"One time, a few of us were sitting together. Everyone boasted of the power he had his hands.

"One person boasted that he has so much power in his hands that when he shoots an arrow, he can pull it back. Even though he already shot the arrow, he can pull it back to him.

"I asked him, 'What kind of an arrow can you pull back?' There are ten types of arrows, depending on the ten types of poisons. If one wants to shoot an arrow, one smears a poison on it. There are ten types of poisons. If one smears the arrow with one poison, the arrow is harmful to a certain degree; and if one smears the arrow with another poison, it is even more harmful. There are ten types of poison, each one worse than the one before it.

---

23. Source: *Sichot Haran*, no. 71.

"I said, 'What kind of arrow can you pull back?'

"I also asked him, 'Can you pull the arrow back before the arrow hits the person, or even after the arrow already hit the person?'

"The other person replied, 'I can pull back one particular type of arrow even after that arrow already hit the person.'

"I said to him, 'If you can only pull back one type of arrow, you cannot heal the princess.'

"Another person boasted that he has so much power in his hands that whenever he takes from someone, he gives to him; he is a charitable man.

"I asked him, 'What kind of charity do you give?'

"He answered, 'I give a tenth.'

"I said, 'If that is so, you cannot heal the princess. Because you give only a tenth, you cannot go to where she is. You can only enter one wall that surrounds her, you cannot go in to her.'

"Another person boasted about the strength in his hands. The leaders—the kings, ministers, and the like—need wisdom. 'I have such power in my hands that I can give each person wisdom with the fact that I support him with my hands.'

"I asked him, 'What kind of wisdom can you give with your hands?' There are ten measures of wisdom.

"He answered, 'I can give one particular type of wisdom.'

"I said, 'If so, you cannot heal the princess, because you cannot know her pulse. There are ten types of pulse. You can only know one pulse, because you can only give one wisdom with your hands.'

"Another person boasted that he has such power in his hands that when there is a storm wind, he can hold it back with his hands. He can grab the wind in his hands and hold it back. More than that, he can control the wind and make it temperate.

"I asked him, 'What kind of wind can you grab? There are ten types of wind.'

"He answered, 'Such and such a wind.'

"I said, 'You cannot heal the princess, for you can cannot play the tune for her. There are ten types of song, and the princess is healed by song. But you can only play one tune for her.'

"They said, 'What can you do?'

"I answered, 'I can do what all of you cannot – that is, the nine parts that each of you cannot do.'

"Here is the story. Once there was a king who desired a princess. He devised all sorts of stratagems to catch her. Finally, he got hold of her, and she stayed with him.

"Once, the king dreamed that she rose up against him and killed him. When he woke up, he was deeply affected by this dream.

"He called all the dream interpreters, and they interpreted it according to its simple meaning: that she would kill him.

"The king didn't know what to do with her.

"Should he kill her? He couldn't bear that.

"Should he send her away? That would bother him very much, for someone else would take her. After he had worked so hard for her, and then she would go to someone else. If he let her go and she went to someone else, she would certainly be able to fulfill the dream and kill him, because she would be with someone else.

"Should he keep her with him? He was afraid that she would kill him.

"So the king didn't know what to do.

"Because of the dream, his love diminished bit by bit and constantly dwindled away. And her love for him also constantly diminished, until she grew to hate him.

"Then she ran away from him.

"The king sent people out to look for her. They reported that she was in the area of the water castle.

"There is a castle made of water, which is surrounded by ten walls one around the other. All ten walls are made of water. The ground in the castle on which one walks is also made of water. The garden, with its trees and fruits, is also made of water. The beauty and uniqueness of the castle cannot be told.

"One cannot enter the castle because, since it is all made of water, one will drown.

"After the princess ran away, she came to the castle, and wandered about it.

"When the king was told that she was wandering around the ware castle, he went with his army to catch her.

"When the princess saw this, she decided to run into the castle; she would rather drown than be caught by the king and have to go back to him. Besides, she may be saved.

"When the king saw her run into the water, he ordered her to be shot—and if she dies, so be it. The soldiers shot, and all ten arrows, which were smeared with ten types of poison, hit her.

"The princess ran into the water castle, passing through all the gates of the watery walls, and got inside. There were gates in the watery walls, and she went through the gates of all ten walls. Finally she entered the castle, and there, she fell down in a faint.

"I can heal her.

"He who does not have all ten types of charity in his hands cannot go through all ten walls of the water castle, for he will drown.

"When the king and his army chased the princess, they were all drowned.

"But I can go through all ten walls of the water castle.

"The walls of water are the waves of the sea that stand like a wall. The winds hold up the waves of the sea, which are the ten walls.

"I can go through all ten walls of the water castle.

"And I can pull out all ten types of arrows. I know all ten pulses through the ten fingers. Through each finger, one can know a separate pulse.

"And I can heal the princess through all ten types of song, for her healing is through song.

"Therefore, I can heal the princess.

"So you see, I have the power in my hands.

"Today I give you this as a gift."

There was great joy, and they were very happy.[24]

---

24. Source: *Sippurei Maasiyot,* "The Seven Beggars," p. 225.

27

Breaking Bad Traits

Free Will

Someone once asked Rabbi Nachman, "What is free will?"

Rabbi Nachman replied simply that free will is in a person's hands. That which he wants to do, he does. That which he doesn't want to do, he doesn't.[1]

≪≪≪

Tanning the Hide

Rabbi Nachman boasted that he had reached the level of breaking desires and bad character traits completely.

He said that there are *tzaddikim* who have broken their desires, but they are like a hide that is being tanned. There still remains a little bit of a bad smell.

He said that one must clean the body the same way one works a hide and turns it inside out. The body must be worked on

---

1. Source: *Likkutei Moharan* 2:110.

completely until one can turn it inside out and see that it is completely clean from all desires and bad character traits.

Rabbi Nachman achieved all of this in his childhood, before he began attaining high achievements, and a great deal of time before he traveled to the land of Israel.

After that journey, he rose higher and higher, from level to level, until he rose to such a high level that one cannot even talk about it.[2]

---

2. Source: *Chayei Moharan* 2:5, no. 5.

28

Money

Taking Care of One's Money

Rabbi Nachman said that when he goes on the road carrying money, he is careful to hide it well in a breast pocket that doesn't have a hole in it. He regularly feels the pocket to make sure he has the money.

Every time one of his followers lost a sum of money on the road and complained to him, he would rebuke him for not having guarded his money carefully.[1]

❦❦❦

Wealth Makes People Crazy

Whoever is wealthy is really crazy.

Money makes him crazy.

This is because money comes from the fall of the wealth of the

---

1. Source: *Chayei Moharan* 2:65, no. 100.

prophets. The Talmud says that all the prophets were wealthy (*Nedarim* 38a).

When a prophet was filled with the spirit of prophecy, he was as though insane. As Rashi explains the verse, "[Saul] prophesied" (1 Samuel 18:10), "He was insane."

When it comes to these wealthy men, the money has turned to complete madness.

Therefore, their wealth has made them mad.[2]

€€€

The Tyranny of Wealth

Some people are immersed in wealth. The more wealth they have, the more worries and depression they have. Their wealth is on the level of "In sorrow shall you eat it" (Genesis 3:19).

But the true *tzaddik* is saved from this.

One needs great wisdom and understanding to keep money from destroying all the days of one's life. The majority of the world is trapped by the lust for money, and money kills them. One can be saved from this only through the *tzaddik*.[3]

---

2. A prophet had to be wealthy. This wealth was a physical manifestation of his connection to spiritual wealth. When he prophesied, he would go into a state of altered consciousness resembling madness.

Wealthy men of today, being attached to their money, also go into a state resembling madness. However, because their attachment is to the money in its this-worldly manifestation, they are, in spiritual terms, insane.

From the point of view of a person to whom spirituality is reality, almost everyone on the planet is insane, because most people treat this world as the only reality.

Source: *Likkutei Moharan* 2:64.

3. Source: *Likkutei Moharan* 1:23:5.

❮❮❮

Wealth Is a Wall

Wealth is a wall. The verse says, "The possessions of a wealthy man are his stronghold, and like a high, tiled wall" (Proverbs 18:11).

Another verse says of anger, "An open city without a wall is a man who cannot control his temper" (Proverbs 28:28).

The concept of a "wall" indicates patience – i.e., overcoming one's anger. Wealth and overcoming one's anger are on the same level, and so they are both called a wall.

When a person damages this wall of wealth with his anger, he turns the wall – *chomah* – into wrath – *cheimah*.

Both wealth and anger stem from the spiritual direction of the left, or the north. One verse says, "The evil will open from the north" (Jeremiah 1:14), and another states, "From the north will come gold" (Job 37:22). [When one faces east, the north is to one's left.]

When a person receives wealth, he has a wall. This wall of wealth stops his anger.

Sometimes, when a person grows angry and he damages the wall of wealth, his anger harms his wealth.

When a person feels overcome with the desire to lose his temper, he should know that at that moment, some measure of money is slated to be granted him from above, and his [evil] inclination wants to ruin this.

One guards oneself by guarding oneself from anger. This is because anger harms one's soul, as in the verse, "He tears his soul in his anger" (Job 18:3). When a person guards himself from anger and builds the wall of wealth, he builds his soul and name. Then all other souls desire to be included within his soul.

This is because the root of all souls is in wealth. As the verse says, "He yearns with all his being for his pay" (Deuteronomy 24:15), which can be literally read as "For its sake he lifts his soul."

That is why if a person steals the money of a Jew, it is as though he has stolen his soul (*Bava Kama* 119a). This is on the level of "[God] will take justice on those who rob a soul" [robbing is like taking a soul] (Proverbs 22:23).

That is why everyone wants to be close to a wealthy man, for the source of their soul is there.[4]

⋘

The Spiritual Source of Money

All souls are drawn to money. They do not only desire and love money, but even the person who has money. It is the nature of people to be drawn after him and to love him because he has money. As the verse says, "Those who love the wealthy are many" (Proverbs 14:20).

This is because the soul comes from a supernal place from which money also devolves.

The spiritual level from which money devolves is a holy place.

Afterward, this influx is corporealized down below and turns into money.

Therefore, the soul desires money, because the soul comes from the same place where money comes from.

But one must not lust for money itself—that is contemptible. Rather, one should long for the place from which the money comes.

In this regard, our sages teach that "Rabi used to honor wealthy men" (*Eiruvin* 86). This is because they have money, which comes from a high place.

All Jews should have money.

But there is one character trait that causes them to lose that money.

This is the evil and contemptible trait of anger. Even if a person wants to be saved from anger—and in particular for the sake of not losing money—it nevertheless overwhelms him

---

4. Source: *Likkutei Moharan* 1:59:5.

from his youth, and he loses the money that should have been his.[5]

_____

5. Everything, including money, has its root in spirituality. The money that we are familiar with on this earth is a physicalization of a primal, spiritual energy. This energy is one of spiritual wealth. When it is corporealized, it turns into money. This energy of spiritual wealth comes from that node in the spiritual network where unimpeded energy is restricted and narrowed, in order that it may be brought down into lower levels of reality. That level is called "severities" – *gevurot*.

A Jew's soul comes from this same level. A soul is divided into several portions. The highest is called *neshamah*, the middle level is *ruach*, and the lowest level is *nefesh*. It is the level of *nefesh* that Rabbi Nachman tells us comes from this same level. In its highest level, a Jew's soul is part of Godliness. But the lowest part of the soul that is manifest in a person as his life force is constricted and then has expression in this world. It too comes from the spiritual area of severities.

Just as one must in general connect all one's thoughts to the spiritual regions, one must be aware of this high aspect of money. But one must not be misled and be drawn after money in its this-worldly manifestation. That is greed. Rather, one must recognize the spiritual root of money, and through the proper use of money serve God. Money is a manifestation of spirituality and thus an important tool for every Jew. Therefore, it is fit that every Jew should be wealthy.

However, this level of severities has a negative aspect as well. Because it constricts spiritual flow, a person's acts can cause not the spiritual flow but the constriction to be brought down into this world.

This destructive constriction manifests itself in this world as anger. When a person is angry, he draws down from the spiritual regions an energy that could have come down either as wealth or anger. Since anger is coming down, wealth cannot.

Rabbi Nachman's implied command – that one should not get angry – is deceptively simple. One can pretend that one is not angry or bypass one's anger without dealing with it, but that does not obviate the anger. To the contrary, via healthy and controlled ventilation of one's anger, one can assuage it and dissipate it. Rabbi Nachman's directives are only meaningful and useful within a larger framework of emotional maturity and health.

Source: *Likkutei Moharan* 1:68.

29

This-Worldly Desires

New Desires

Rabbi Nachman said that nowadays the desire for wealth, influence, and honor is greater than unrefined sexual desire.

Even the most inconsequential people, such as coachmen and the like, make money into a goal. Whatever money they earn they send home to their wives in order to amass it, and they do not spend it for their desires (editor's note: as they used to), for this desire for money and influence is now greater than sexual desire.[1]

❮❮❮

The Country of Wealth

There was a country that had a great deal of wealth. All the people were wealthy. But the custom of the country was very strange. Everything was judged by wealth. Everyone's level of honor was determined by his wealth. A law was passed that if a

---

1. Source: *Chayei Moharan* 2:52, no. 25.

person had a certain amount of money, he was given a certain degree of honor. If he had another amount of money, he was given another degree of honor. Everything depended on the amount of money that a person had. A person who had a very large amount of money became the king.[2]

⋘

The Countries of This-Worldly Desire

It was written in their chronicles that there had once been a great storm. This storm had turned over the entire world. It had turned sea into dry land and dry land into sea, desert into inhabited land and inhabited land into desert. It had mixed up the entire world. After this confusion, when the entire world was mixed up, the people of the world decided to choose a king. They decided that whoever is working on fulfilling the purpose of the world should be king. So they started pondering, "What is the purpose of the world?"

There were a number of opinions.

One group of people said that the purpose of the world is honor. We see that everyone believes that honor is the most important thing. If a person isn't given honor, if he is spoken to disrespectfully, he can spill blood. Also, after a person's death, his body is guarded with honor, buried with honor, and so on.

After death, one no longer wants money. Nevertheless, people are careful to honor him.

This group of people came up with other such logic and reasons to prove that honor is the purpose of the world. They decided to search for a person who runs after honor. That person should be made king.

They went searching for such a person. They saw an old gypsy beggar being carried about and followed by about five hundred people. The beggar was blind, bent over, and deaf. The people who were following him were members of his family—he had many sisters and brothers and they had many children. The old

---

2. Source: *Sippurei Maasiyot,* "The Master of Prayer," p. 142.

beggar was very strict about his honor. He was very short-tempered, and he was constantly getting angry at them. Because he chased so much after honor, he was given a great deal of respect.

So this group of people appointed him to be their king.

Another group said that the purpose of the world is murder. We see that everything in the world decays. Everything – grass, fruits, people, and so on – ultimately rots away. So the purpose of all things is eventual destruction. A murderer, who kills and destroys people, brings the world to its purpose. So they concluded that the purpose is murder.

They searched for an angry and jealous murderer, thinking that such a person should be king.

They heard yelling. They asked, "What is it?"

They were told, "Someone has killed his father and mother."

They exclaimed, "Who can equal such a murderer, a man who has such a strong heart and who is so cruel that he can kill his own father and mother? Such a man has reached the purpose."

He pleased this group of people very much, and they appointed him king.

Another group said that a person who eats a great deal of gourmet foods should be king. But they couldn't find such a person. In the meantime, they chose a wealthy man who ate a lot (and whose food was somewhat refined), until they would be able to find the person they wanted. They made him king until they would be able to find the person they really wanted.

Another group said that a beautiful woman should be king, for the purpose of the world is that it should be populated (for the world was created for this reason). A beautiful woman awakens desire, which increases the world's population, and brings it to its purpose. They found a beautiful woman and made her their king.

Others said that the purpose of the world is speech. Speech marks the difference between a human being and an animal. Because this is what makes a person superior to an animal, it comprises the purpose of the world. They searched for an eloquent speaker who knows several languages and who constantly talks. They found a crazy Frenchman who was walking and talking to himself. They asked him if he knows languages. He knew a few languages, and so they decided that he had certainly reached the goal. He pleased them, and they appointed him king.

Another group said that the purpose of the world is joy. When a child is born, people are joyous; if there is a wedding, people are joyous; when a country is conquered, people are joyous. So everyone's purpose is joy. Therefore, they looked for a person who was always joyous. Such a person no doubt reached the goal, and should be their king. They saw a Gentile in a dirty shirt carrying a bottle of whiskey, being followed by several other Gentiles. This man was very joyous, because he was very drunk. When they saw that he was so joyous and had no worries, he pleased them very much, for he had attained the purpose of the world, which is joy. So they made the Gentile their king. And he certainly led them on the straight path.

Others said that the purpose of the world is wisdom. So they searched for a very wise man and made him king.

Some said that the purpose of the world is to concentrate on eating and drinking and to grow large limbs (muscles). They looked for a large person with large limbs, and who exercised to enlarge his limbs. Since he was so large, he had a bigger portion of the world, for he took up more room, and he was thus closer to the purpose of the world, which is to make one's limbs bigger. Such a person should be king. They went and they found a tall athlete. They were pleased with him, for he had large limbs, and so he had attained the goal of the world: and so they made him their king.

But there was another group that said that all these things are not the goal at all. The true goal is only to pray to God, to be humble and small, and so on. These people looked for a prayer leader and they appointed him as their king.[3]

---

3. Source: *Sippurei Maasiyot*, "The Master of Prayer," p. 162.

30

This World

The Purpose of This World

The only point of this world is to draw one to one's ultimate purpose.

One shouldn't be concerned whether or not one has money. Either way, one will live his life the same way.[1]

This world fools us completely. It makes a person think that he is constantly earning. But in the end he has nothing. Most people, who work for years in business and trade, in the end have nothing to show for it. Even if a person does accumulate money, it is taken away from him.

A man and his money cannot remain together. Either the money is taken from the man, or the man is taken from the money. But one never finds that a person remains together with his money.

Also, where is all the money that has been earned since the creation of the world? For all of creation, people have been making money. And where is it all? The truth is that money is nothing at all.[2]

---

1. This refers not to basic necessities but to luxuries.
2. Source: *Sichot Haran*, no. 51.

€€€

The Harvest of Tainted Wheat

Once, a king told his friend, the prime minister, "As an astrologer, I see that whoever eats any of the wheat that grows this year will go mad. Let us think of some solution."

The prime minister answered, "Let us have some of last year's wheat set aside for us so that we will not have to eat the tainted grain."

The king replied, "If we do this, we alone will be sane in a mad world. Then it will be as though we are the ones who are mad and the others sane. But it isn't possible to set wheat aside for everyone either. So we will also have to eat the tainted wheat. But we shall make a mark on our foreheads, so that when we look at each others' foreheads, we will know that we are mad."[3]

€€€

It Were Better Not to Have Been Created

"Our sages said that "it were better for a person not have been created" (*Eirachin* 13b). Also, the verse says, "Better than both [those alive and those who have died] is the one that still has not been" (Ecclesiastes 4:3).

This is extraordinary. If this is so, why was man created?

These words only refer to this world. People suffer so many sorrows and troubles in this world that it would have been better if they had not been created.

But when one takes into account the world-to-come, it is

---

3. One cannot be in the world without taking its illusions to be reality. Even the *tzaddik* must enter this-worldly reality for the purpose of helping others. But the *tzaddik* and his followers form a community in which they can remind themselves that this-worldly reality is illusory. Just as the follower needs the *tzaddik* to do this, so does the *tzaddik* need the follower.

Source: *Avanehah Barzel*, p. 27.

better that people were created, for one can come to the
ultimate purpose.

As for this world, "better is one hour of repentance and good
deeds in this world than the entire life of the world-to-come"
(*Avot*, chap. 4).[4]

€€€

To Laugh at the World

Rabbi Nachman told someone that he had had the idea of taking
his wife, traveling far away, and living anonymously. He would
go to the marketplace occasionally and laugh at the entire
world.[5]

€€€

Hidden in a Fist

The evil inclination is like a person who runs among people with
his hand closed. No one knows what he is holding. He holds out
his hand and asks everyone, "What am I carrying?"

Everyone imagines that this person is carrying what he desires.

Everyone runs after him, for everyone believes that he is
holding what one wants.

Then the man opens his hand at last, and there is nothing
there.

The desires of this world are like sunbeams shining into a
house. People want to grasp them, but they grasp nothing.[6]

---

4. This world has justification and joy only insofar as it connects to
the world-to-come. But if only this world existed, it would have been
better that it had never been created.
Source: *Likkutei Moharan* 2:39.
5. Source: *Chayei Moharan* 2:10, no. 19.
6. Source: *Sichot Haran*, no. 6.

⋘

Do Not Let the World Fool You

Do not let the world fool you. There is no one whom this world brings to a good end. All those who held the entire world in their hands came to a bad end, and they even ruined things for generations to come. Even non-Jews know this.

This is because there is no this-worldly reality.

What does one have to do? One needs mercy from heaven to know what one must do.

But a Jew doesn't need this. A Jew already knows what to do from the Torah.[7]

⋘

A Little Coin before the Mountain

The world stands before a person's eyes and keeps him from seeing the light of the Torah and the *tzaddikim*, a light that is greater than the world by thousands and tens of thousands of degrees. But if a person turns his eyes and lifts his head and looks higher than the barrier of this world, he will see the great light of the Torah and *tzaddikim*.

This world is like a little coin that is before one's eyes and blocks out a great mountain. One can easily move the coin aside and see the mountain.[8]

---

7. When one realizes that this-worldly reality is illusory, one is faced with the dilemma of how to conduct oneself. Only a supernatural consciousness that surveys this reality from the outside can inform a person of the proper way to act—"one needs mercy from heaven to know what one must do."

But a Jew already has the Torah. The Torah informs a Jew how to act in an ultimately meaningful way in this physical world.

Source: *Sichot Haran*, no. 51.

8. Source: *Likkutei Moharan* 2:119.

€€€

"This World" Does Not Exist

Rabbi Nachman spoke with us a number of times about the suffering of this world. He said that everyone in this world is filled with suffering, and that there is not one person who has this world.

Even the richest people, even the leaders, do not have this world.

All their days are filled with anguish.

They are all filled with troubles, worries, and depression. Each one has his own troubles.

Not one lord or minister has everything the way he wants it at every moment.

All these people are filled with constant trouble and worries.

This is clear to anyone who knows anything about them and their lives.

Even if it appears that someone has this world with its pleasures of wealth, honor, palaces, beautiful things, jewelry, and fancy clothing, a clear look will reveal that he too is filled with a great deal of trouble and worry.

Everyone says that there is this world and the world-to-come. We believe in the world-to-come and it is also possible that a "this world" exists some place. But we see that our existence here is in purgatory, because everyone here is filled with great suffering all the time. There is no "this world" at all.[9]

---

9. Because this world in itself has so many troubles, because all joys that have no transcendental aspect cannot give a purposeful delight, and because the most trouble-free existence is filled with many worries and pains, this world, denuded of any transcendental significance, is a world that has so much pain that it could be called purgatory. As for a "this world," a world in which one neither suffers nor enjoys bliss, that is a neutral environment that does not exist.

Source: *Likkutei Moharan* 2:119.

31

Health

Health Is Paramount

Rabbi Nachman said, "When a person is healthy, he must do and do and do (to serve God). And when a person isn't well, everything must be set aside (and he should only engage in the minimal service of God as ordered by the *Shulchan Aruch* in accordance with the state of his health). One must keep the *mitzvah* of 'Take very good care of yourselves.' "[1]

⋘

Health and Medicine

Imagine someone who was very much needed by the world. But he was grabbed, put into a room, and told, "Stay here!"

[Similarly,] I was taken and put on the third or fourth floor, very high up.

I used to be like a merchant who goes to the market with

---

1. Source: *Avanehah Barzel*, p. 44, no. 6.

many things to do. Even when I was told that I need to rest and relax, I didn't pay any attention. What is rest and relaxation? One only has to work constantly, constantly.

But now that I am ill, I have to guard my eating, my sleeping, and so on.

I had a good body that didn't demand anything of me or bother me at all. But now I have to watch what time I eat, and the like. It is impossible to describe my sufferings – I am referring to mental anguish, of course.

I have taken medicines and drunk henna. In China, from which henna comes, the people are total heretics who claim that there is "no Judge and no justice."

I took other medicines from other places in which there are other heretics. When all this went into me, a process took place.[2]

---

2. It was necessary that the medicine that came from there should go into Rabbi Nachman for him to subjugate the heresy.

Source: *Chayei Moharan* 1:74, no. 14.

32

Exile

Raising the Fallen Places

Our sages said, "Wherever the [Jews] go, they evenutally become rulers over their masters" (*Sanhedrin* 104a).

Wherever Jews go in the exile, they are at first oppressed, but they eventually rule over their former masters, for they take over the place.

This is because the Jews raise all low and fallen places. Our sages said, "With the coming of the messiah, the theaters and circuses will be filled with people learning Torah. As the verse says, [speaking of the conversion of the Philistines to Judaism,] 'they will also remain [faithful] to our God' (Zechariah 9:7) (*Megillah* 6a)."

The Jews in exile are called "people of the exile" [a phrase used in the book of Ezra]. Even though they afterward become masters and raise everything up, they are nevertheless initially in exile. Only after traveling through exile do they raise everything.

The word *exile—golah—*forms the acronym for "they will also remain [faithful] to our God." This is because ultimately the Jews raise everything. This is seen in the fact that the pagan Philistines converted and that in the future, theaters and circuses will be consecrated to Torah study.[1]

❦❦❦

The Golden Mountain and the Pearl Castle

On the road, I told a story, and whoever heard it had an impulse to repent.

This is the story.

Once upon a time, there was a king.

The king had six sons and one daughter.

He thought very highly of his daughter. He loved her very much, and he took great delight in her.

One time, when he was together with her, he grew angry at her. The words, "May the Evil One take you away!" flew out of his mouth.

That night, the princess went to her room. The next morning, no one knew where she was.

Her father was filled with anguish, and he went around searching for her. When the king's minister saw the king's anguish, he stood up and asked to be given a servant, a horse, and money for expenses. He then set off to search for her.

He searched a great deal and for a very long time, until he found her.

This is the story of his search.

He traveled for a long time through deserts, fields, and forests.

When he went through one desert, he saw a side road. He thought, "Since I have been traveling for such a long time in the desert and I haven't been able to find her, I will take that road. Perhaps it will lead to a town."

He traveled for a long while. Finally, he saw a fortress surrounded by many soldiers.

Both the fortress and soldiers surrounding it were very handsome.

---

1. Source: *Likkutei Moharan* 2:76.

He was afraid that the soldiers would not let him in. Still, he decided that he would try.

Leaving the horse behind, he went to the fortress.

The soldiers let him in. No one made a move to stop him. He went from room to room, and no one bothered him.

He came to a palace. He saw the king sitting, wearing his crown, as many soldiers stood about him.

Many musicians were playing on instruments, and it was quite beautiful.

Neither the king nor anyone else asked him anything.

He saw good food there, and so he ate. He went to a corner and lay down to see what would happen next.

The king give an order that the queen be brought out, and people went to get her.

As the queen was brought out, there was a commotion and great joy, and the musicians played and sang.

The queen was placed on a throne next to the king.

When the minister saw the queen, he recognized her.

The queen noticed that someone was lying in a corner. When she looked closer, she recognized him. She stood up from the throne, went over to him, and touched him. She asked him, "Do you know who I am?"

"Yes, I know you. You are the princess who disappeared. How do you come to be here?"

"I am here because of those words that flew out of my father's mouth. This is the place of evil."

The minister told the princess that her father was filled with anguish, and that he, the minister, had been searching for her for many years.

He asked her, "How can I rescue you?"

She answered, "You can only rescue me if you find a place to sit for one year. For that entire year, you should only sit and yearn for me. If you do that, then you will be able to free me. When you have time, you should only yearn and desire and hope to take me out. And you should fast. On the last day of the year, you should fast and not sleep for the entire twenty-four hours."

He went and did this. At the end of the year, on the very last

day, he fasted and didn't sleep. Then he got up and set out for the
princess. On the way, he saw a tree on which grew very beautiful
apples. They were so beautiful that he went over and ate from
them.

As soon as he ate from the apple, he fell into a sleep. He slept
for a very long time.

His servant tried to wake him up, but he could not. Finally,
the minister awoke.

He asked his servant, "Where am I in the world?"

His servant told him the whole story. "You have been sleeping
for a very long while. A few years have already passed. In the
meantime, I lived by eating these fruits."

The minister was filled with anguish. He went over to the
fortress and found the princess there.

She poured her heart out to him bitterly and in great sadness.
"Because of one day, you lost everything. If you had come on
that day, you would have taken me out. I know that not to eat is
very hard, and particularly on the last day. Then the evil
inclination is very strong.

"You should again choose a spot, and you should again sit
there for a year. This time, on the last day, you may eat. But you
may not sleep. And you should not drink any wine in order that
you not fall asleep, for sleep is the most important thing."

He went and did all that she said. On the last day, he set out
for her. On the way there, he saw a spring running. The spring
was colored red and smelled like wine. He asked his servant, "Do
you see that? This is a spring, but it is colored red, and it smells
like wine!"

He went and tasted the spring.

He immediately fell down and slept for seventy years.

Many soldiers passed by with their belongings following after
them. The servant hid himself from the soldiers. Then a carriage
passed by, inside of which sat the princess.

When she passed by the minister, she stepped down and sat
next to him. She recognized him and tried very hard to wake him
up. But he could not get up.

She began to rebuke him: "After so much effort and hard
work, after so many years that you ran yourself ragged to rescue

me, for the sake of one day you couldn't rescue me. You spoiled everything." And she cried bitterly.

She said, "It is a great pity on both of us. I have been here for so long, and I cannot get out."

She took her kerchief from her head and wrote on it with her tears. She put it next to him. Then she got up and went back to the carriage, and she rode away.

Afterward, the minister woke up. He asked his servant, "Where am I in the world?"

The servant told him the entire story of all the soldiers who had passed by, of the carriage, and how the princess had cried over him, and that she had said, "It is a great pity on both of us," and so on.

The minister noticed the kerchief next to him. He asked his servant, "Where is this from?"

His servant answered, "She wrote on it with her tears and left it."

The minister took the kerchief and had held it up to the sun.

He began to see the letters. He read her complaint and outcry that were written there.

He also read that she was no longer in the fortress. He should search for golden mountain with a palace of pearls. "There you will find me," she wrote.

The minister left his servant behind and went to look for her on his own.

He searched for a few years.

Being an expert in maps, he concluded that there was no golden mountain and pearl palace in any populated areas. He decided that he would go and look for her in the deserts, and he spent many years searching for her there.

One day, he saw an inhumanly tall giant, who was carrying a great tree. One could never find such a large tree in a populated area. The giant asked him, "Who are you?"

"I am a man."

The giant was astonished at this. He said, "I have been in the desert a long time, but I have never seen a man."

The minister told him the entire story of his search for a golden mountain and a pearl palace.

The giant answered, "There is no such thing." He discouraged
the minister and told him, "You were told nonsense. There isn't
any such thing."

The minister began to weep with great feeling. "There is such
a thing!" he insisted. "It must exist somewhere!"

The giant again discouraged him. "You were told nonsense."

But the minister said, "It certainly exists somewhere."

So the giant told him, "I think this is all nonsense. But since
you are so stubborn, I will you do a favor. I am in charge of all
the animals. I will call the animals that run across the entire
world to see if any of them knows about this mountain and
palace."

He called all the animals from small to great, and questioned
them, and they all answered that they had never seen any such
thing.

He told the minister, "You see, you were told nonsense. If you
would listen to me, you would go back home. You will certainly
not find this, because it doesn't exist."

But the minister grew very stubborn and insisted, "It must
exist!"

The giant told him, "I have a brother in the desert who is in
charge of all the birds. Maybe they know about this golden
mountain and pearl palace. Since they fly high up in the air,
maybe they saw the mountain and palace. Go to him and tell him
I sent you."

The minister traveled for a few years and searched until he
found another giant, who also carried a giant tree. This giant
questioned him as the first one had and he answered him as he
had before, adding that his brother had sent him.

This giant also discouraged the minister, and told him that
such a thing doesn't exist.

But the minister replied that such a place definitely does exist.

The giant told him, "I am in charge of all the birds. I will call
them. Perhaps they know." He called together all the birds, and
questioned them all, from small to great.

The birds answered that they didn't know of such a mountain
and palace.

The giant told the minister, "You see, it definitely doesn't exist. If you would listen to me, you would go back. This doesn't exit."

But the minister grew stubborn and said, "It certainly does exist."

The giant told him, "Farther on in the desert lives my brother who is in charge of all the winds that blow across the entire world. Perhaps they know about this."

So the minister traveled and searched for several years, until he found another giant who also carried a great tree. This giant asked him the same questions as before, and the minister answered him and told him the entire story.

This giant also discouraged the minister, but the minister pleaded with him. The giant told him that he would do him a favor and call all the winds and question them. He called all the winds, and questioned them, but no one knew of the mountain and the palace.

The giant told the minister, "You see, you were told nonsense."

But the minister began to cry, saying, "I know for sure that it exists."

In the meantime, one more wind arrived. The giant rebuked it, "Why are you so late? I commanded all the winds to come. Why didn't you come together with them?"

The wind replied, "I was late because I had to carry a princess to a golden mountain with a pearl palace."

The minister was overjoyed.

The giant asked the wind, "What is expensive there?"

The wind replied, "There, everything is expensive."

The giant said to the minister, "You have been searching a very long time for her, and you have worked very hard. It is possible that now you will have a problem because of money. So I will give you a pot. Whenever you put your hand in the pot, you will take out money." He then told the wind to carry the minister there. The storm wind came and carried the minister to the mountain and brought him to the door [of the town].

Soldiers were standing there, and they didn't let him into the town. He put his hand into the pot and took out money. He bribed the soldiers, and went into the town.

It was a beautiful town. He went to a wealthy man and bought food from him. He saw that he would have to remain there a long time, and he would have to use his wisdom and intelligence to rescue the princess.

Rabbi Nachman did not tell how the minister rescued her.
But in the end, he did free her.
Amen Selah.[2]

2. Source: *Sippurei Maasiyot*, "Story of the Lost Princess," p. 1.

33

Unifying Both Worlds

One Must Leave a Blessing Behind

When a man dies, his soul rises and clings to its level in the upper worlds.

But it is not the ultimate purpose that the soul should only cling to the supernal worlds. The perfection of the soul is that while it is above, it is also below.

A person must leave a blessing behind him—a son or a student—in order that his understanding remain down below at the time that his soul rises up. As our sages said, " 'They have no one to take their place' (Psalms 55:20)—one rabbi said this refers to a son, and another said it refers to a student" (*Bava Batra* 116a).

Both the student and son receive the understanding of their teacher and father. It is no advantage if the son is wicked, God forbid; one should leave behind a son who is on the level of being a student, who will receive one's wisdom and understanding.[1]

---

1. Source: *Likkutei Moharan* 2:7:4.

﹩﹩﹩

The *Tzaddik* Is on All Levels

The wise man who reaches the transcendental energies, the energy flow from the divine Crown, must have the level of "all." This is related to the verse, "All in the heavens and in the earth" (1 Chronicles 29:11), whose Aramaic translation is "Who unites heaven and earth" (*Zohar* Genesis 31, *Tikkun* 22).

This person should be able to grasp and maintain both the supernal and lower world, which are the levels of heaven and earth.

The wise *tzaddik* must grasp both and maintain each one on its level.

There are some who dwell above on the level of the supernal world and heaven, and some who dwell below on the level of the lower world and earth.

The *tzaddik* must show those who dwell above that they [ultimately] know nothing of God. This is the awareness of "what," as in the phrase, "What did you see, what did you examine?" This is the level of "Where is the place of His glory?" (Prayer book).

The *tzaddik* must show those who dwell below that "the world is full of His glory" (Isaiah 6:3).

There are people who dwell in the dust, people who are on the lowest level and who imagine that they are very far from God. The *tzaddik* must awaken them, as in the verse, "Awake and sing, dwellers in the dust" (Isaiah 26:19). He must make it clear to them that God is with them and that they are close to Him, for "the world is full of His glory." He must strengthen them and raise them from despair, for they are close to God, because the entire world is filled with His glory.

This is the level of "all" that the *tzaddik* possesses, the level of "all in the heavens and earth" that "unites heaven and earth." He grasps and maintains the two worlds, the upper world on the level of "what" and "where is the place of His glory"; and the lower world on the level of "The entire world is filled with His glory."[2]

❮❮❮

In Two Worlds at Once

On the first day of Hannukah, 5569 (1798), after lighting the Hannukah *menorah*, a guest entered the house.

He asked the man who lived there, "How do you support yourself?"

The man answered, "I don't have a regular income in my house. I am supported by the world."

The guest asked, "What are you learning?" and the man answered him.

They began speaking with each other, until they began to speak words that come from the heart.

The man who lived there began to yearn a great deal to know how one arrives at a certain level of holiness.

The guest told him, "I will learn with you."

The man of the house was amazed, and he began to think, "Perhaps this guest isn't a human being at all." But when he saw that the guest was talking with him like a human being, his faith in him as a human being was strengthened.

He immediately began to call the guest Rabbi, and he told him, "First of all, I want to learn how to treat you with the proper respect, and certainly how not to insult you. But it is difficult for a creature of flesh and blood to be completely careful. Please teach me how to treat you with the proper respect."

The guest replied, "I don't have time right now. Another time, I will come and teach you this. But now I have to leave."

The man said, "Tell me how far I should accompany you."

The guest replied, "Until past the door."

The man began to think, "How can I go out with him? Right now, I'm among others (because there were other people in the house). But should I go out with him alone? Who knows who he really is?" He said aloud, "I'm afraid to go out with you."

---

2. Source: *Likkutei Moharan* 2:7:7.

The guest replied, "Since I can learn with you, if I wanted to do anything to you even now, who could stop me?"

The man accompanied his guest past the door. The guest immediately grabbed the man and they began to fly. The man was cold, so the guest took a garment and gave it to him. He told him, "Take this garment; it will be good for you. You will have to eat and drink, and you will sit in your house." And he flew with him.

When the man looked around, he saw that he was in his house. He himself didn't believe that he was in his house. But he saw that he was speaking with people and eating and drinking.

In the middle of that, he saw that he was flying as before. Then he saw that he was in his house again. Then he was flying. This continued for a long time.

The guest brought him down in a valley between two mountains. He found a book there that was filled with combinations of letters: *aleph, zayin, chet*, and *dalet*, and so on. There were illustrations of vessels, and inside the vessels were letters. Also, inside the vessels were the letters referring to those vessels – that is, using those letters, one could make those vessels. The man had a great desire to learn that book.

He looked and saw that he was back in his house. Again he looked and he was in the valley.

He decided to go up the mountain. Perhaps he would find a community there. When he climbed up the mountain, he saw a golden tree with golden branches. On the branches hung vessels like those that had been illustrated in the book. Inside these vessels were tools by means of which one made the vessels.

He wanted to take the vessels. But he couldn't, because they were entangled in the crooked branches.

Meanwhile, he saw that he was back in his house.

He found this extraordinary. How was it that he was one moment here and one moment there?

He wanted to tell this to the people in the house, but how could he tell them such an incredible thing?

Meanwhile, he looked out the window and saw the guest. He began to plead with the guest to come to him.

The guest said, "I don't have time, because I am going to you."

The man said, "This itself is incredible. I'm here, and what do you mean that you are going to me?"

The guest answered, "At the moment that you agreed to accompany me past the door, I took your *neshamah* – the highest level of your soul – and gave it a garment from the lower *Gan Eden*, leaving you your two lower soul levels of *nefesh* and *ruach*. When you bring your thought to your *neshamah*, you are there and you draw down an illumination from there to you here. But when you return here, you are here."

I don't know what world he is from. But he is certainly from a good world.

And the story has still not come to its end.[3]

---

3. Source: *Chayei Moharan* 1:39, no. 5.

34

The Gradual Process of Redemption

The World Is Improving

Rabbi Nachman said that God's way is different than that of man. After a person makes a garment, he cares for it as long as it is new. But as it gets older, it spoils, and he doesn't think so much of it.

But when God created the world, it was spoiled at first. Then, step by step, it was rectified and He regarded it more highly.

Then came Abraham, Isaac, and Jacob, and afterward Moses. Step by step, *tzaddikim* rectify the world. Continuously, the world becomes more precious to God. Finally, the Messiah will come and the world will be perfected.[1]

❮❮❮

Spiritual Evolution

Rabbi Nachman spoke of the kings who war against each other and spill a great deal of blood for nothing. He said that a number

---

1. Source: *Sichot Haran*, no. 239.

of follies (such as human sacrifice) that people used to believe in in previous generations have already been eradicated.

But the error of war has not been eradicated.

He said, "These people use their wisdom to make a weapon that can kill thousands of people at one blow. But can there be any greater idiocy than destroying many lives for nothing?"[2]

---

2. Source: *Chayei Moharan* 2:64, no. 99.

35

The Purpose

Reaching the Ultimate Goal

A person must work very hard to reach the ultimate goal. Right now, the physical nature of the world and other obstacles prevent one from really understanding the reason that one has to come close to a *tzaddik*.

But after death, people will understand what they had previously heard and what they will hear then, in particular, things that relate to the soul.

And what if, even then, a person cannot come close to the *tzaddik*. . . ?

The main thing is that everyone should be strong in his faith in God and in the true *tzaddik*, and he should do all that the *tzaddik* says. Then he will not be ashamed in either this world or the world-to-come.[1]

❦❦❦

---

1. Source: *Chayei Moharan* 1:47, no. 21.

The Ultimate Purpose

1. Everything has a purpose. That purpose has yet another purpose, and so on, higher and higher.

For instance, the purpose of building a house is so that a person will have a place to rest. And the purpose of resting is to have strength to serve God.

2. The purpose of creation is the delight of the world to come.[2]

᚛᚛᚛

In the Ultimate Places

I heard from a Bratslaver that Rabbi Nachman told him this story on the eve of Yom Kippur, after *kaparot*.

Rabbi Nachman told that he was walking in a forest. The forest was large and without end, and he wanted to go back. Someone came to him and told him that it is impossible to come to the end of this forest, because it has no end. All the vessels in the world are made from this forest. But he showed Rabbi Nachman a way to get out of the forest.

Afterward, Rabbi Nachman came to a river, and he wanted to come to the end of the river. Again, someone came to him and told him that one cannot come to the end of this river, because this river has no end. All the people in the world drink from the waters of this river.

But he showed Rabbi Nachman a way to get to the end of the river.

Then Rabbi Nachman came to a mill that was standing by the river. Again someone came to him and told him that this mill grinds the grain for the entire world.

Then he went back to the forest, and he saw a blacksmith

---

2. Source: *Likkutei Moharan* 1:18.

sitting in the forest and working. He was told that that blacksmith made the tools for the entire world.

These matters are very mysterious.

(This wasn't recorded in its entirety, for much was forgotten,
since it wasn't written immediately.)

He said then, "The world tells a story, but I have seen a
story."[3]

---

3. Source: *Chayei Moharan* 1:44, no. 15.

36

Living Off Wisdom

The Level of the Patriarchs

On Rabbi Nachman's return from the Land of Israel, he and his companion were traveling on a warship, two Jews alone on a vessel manned by many Arabs. It is the custom of Arabs—and especially of Arab soldiers—to capture Jews and sell them as slaves in distant lands. Rabbi Nachman was very much frightened of this.

He began to think, What would he do if he were taken to some far-away place where no Jews live, and sold there? Who would know of it?

He fell into great anguish: How would he be able to perform the *mitzvot*? Finally, he realized that he could serve God even if it were impossible for him to keep the *mitzvot*, God forbid. He realized the level of service that the patriarchs experienced before the giving of the Torah. They kept the *mitzvot*, although not in the simple sense. For instance, Jacob kept the *mitzvah* of *tefillin* via the branches that he peeled (Genesis 30:37; *Zohar* 1:162b). Rabbi Nachman realized how to keep all the *mitzvot* in this way if he were to be taken and sold in such a place, God forbid.

209

As soon as Rabbi Nachman realized this, God helped him, and another ship arrived upon the scene.[1]

⋘

Without Eating or Drinking

Rabbi Nachman said that there are high and awesome wisdoms, even in this world, from which a person could live without eating and drinking.[2]

⋘

Rising to the Ultimate Level

Every spiritual level and every universe contains the two categories of "we will do and we will listen" (Exodus 24:7). Everyone has both these levels. "We will do" is Torah—i.e., those things that are revealed to one. "We will hear" is the level of hidden things, or prayer.

When a person comes to a higher level, then his "hearing" is transformed into "doing," and he attains a new level of "hearing."

And so it goes from level to level.

Similarly, each universe has the concepts of "we will do and we will hear."

That which is on the level of "we will hear" for this world is on the level of "we will do" for the next higher world, and that world has a higher level of "we will hear."

So it goes from world to world.

This is referred to in the phrase, "The Torah of God and his Torah" (Psalms 1:2) (*Avodah Zarah* 19a).[3]

---

1. Source: *Shivchei Haran*, Rabbi Nachman's Journey to the Land of Israel, p. 23.

2. Source: *Sichot Haran*, no. 306.

3. The Talmud states that at first the Torah was called after the name of God. But in the end, it is called after the name of the student

At first it is called "the Torah of God," which is hidden – "the hidden things are to the Lord our God" (Deuteronomy 29:28). Afterward, when a person rises to a higher level, this becomes "his Torah." The "hearing" has been transformed into "doing," which is the level of "and the revealed things are for us and our children" (Deuteronomy 29:28).[4]

This is referred to in the verse, "The hidden things are for the Lord our God [the level of 'hearing'] forever to do all the words of this Torah" (Deuteronomy 29:28) – "doing." A person should go from level to level and come to the world in which "hearing" is transformed into "doing."

This is referred to in the words *to do all the words of this Torah.* "The words of the Torah" are the words that surround the actual *mitzvah*, such as "And God said." These words are on the level of "hearing." They will be transformed into the level of "doing."

This is referred to by the word "forever" – a person will go from level to level and from world to world ("forever" literally means "until the world").

"To do" refers to the level of doing "all the words of this Torah" – these words surround the *mitzvah*, which is the level of hidden things, of "hearing." These words will be transformed into "doing" the revealed things.

Every individual must go from level to level and from world to world until he arrives at a higher level of "let us do and let us hear." His "doing" must be constantly formed from the previous level of "hearing." The level of hiddenness, prayer, words of Torah surrounding the *mitzvah*, "the Torah of God" must be transformed into the level of "we will do," the level of revealed

---

who has studied it. As the verse says, "In the Torah of God is his delight, and in his Torah he will speak day and night" (Psalms 1:2).

4. Torah must be internalized. The ultimate proof that one understands and embodies Torah is not through a demonstration of one's understanding but through one's acts. At first, the Torah is God's. In that form, Torah is an external authority imposed on a person.

This is not a mature level. A person must internalize and integrate the Torah into his person so that the Torah becomes his.

things, Torah, "His Torah." The person will then be given a higher level of "hearing." He must rise from level to level until he comes to the very first point of creation, the beginning of Emanation.

At that point, there is also a concept of "we will do and we will hear." The level there of "we will hear" is the true Torah of God. On every other level, the "Torah of God" is only called so by analogy; it is called the Torah of God because it is hidden from the person. Then, when one person gets to that level, it is called one's own Torah. But the level of "we will hear" at the beginning of Emanation is truly the Torah of God. There is nothing higher. This is the actual Torah of God.[5]

Afterward, when a person clings to the Infinite One, the "doing" is on the level of the actual Torah of God, and the "hearing" is the level of the actual prayer of God.

There is a Torah of God. As our sages said, "God says, I kept [the Torah] first" (*Bechorim* and *Rosh Hashanah*); "God clothes the naked and visits the sick, etc." (*Sotah* 14a); and "From where do we know that God wears phylacteries?" (*Berachot* 6a).

There is also a prayer of God. As our sages said, "How do we know that God prays? The verse says, 'You shall rejoice in the house of My prayer' (Isaiah 56:7) (*Berachot* 7a)."

We see that there is a Torah of God and prayer of God.

When a person clings to the Infinite One, his Torah is the Torah of God, and his prayer is the prayer of God.

This is related to our sages' statement that "when a person prays for compassion for someone else and he himself needs the same thing, he is answered first" (*Bava Kamma* 92a). Although he needs the same thing, he doesn't pray for it because he is on the level of nothingness, which is the level of the beginning that precedes creation. Since he is on the level of beginning, he is answered first. . . .[6]

---

5. God is said to have looked into the Torah and created the world. This is the Torah of God, the template for the creation of the rest of the universe.

6. Source: *Likkutei Moharan* 1:22:10.

€€€

Apprehending the Ultimate

The universe that God created contains so many wonderful things – how great are the works of God!

Even in this world alone, God's wonders are great. He created inanimate matter, plants, and so on. Who can fathom God's greatness in the nature of this world alone, not to mention in the other worlds?

Everything was only created for the sake of Israel.

The purpose of the creation of Israel itself was for the sake of Shabbat.

Shabbat is the purpose of the creation of heaven and earth; it is the world of souls (Introduction to *Zohar* 1b and *Zohar Terumah* 136), a world that is entirely Shabbat.

When this stage is reached, people will apprehend God correctly without any dividing barrier. There will be a complete oneness. Everyone will point with his finger, saying, "This is God for Whom we have hoped" (*Taanit* 31a).

This is the purpose for which God created the entire creation.

Everything in the world has in it a level of this purpose. Everything in the world has a beginning and an end. The beginning is the spiritual level from which it came down until it took on physical form. The end is the purpose for which it was created.

The people of Israel are capable of looking deeply into the details of creation and seeing in them God's greatness and in this way serving Him.

And this is so even when [they examine everything] in its highest aspects, until the ultimate level, where that detail comes to its fulfillment.

Everything contains a part of the purpose for which it was created, via which one can reach God and serve Him.

Every individual must look deeply into this to be able to recognize the greatness of the Creator in everything, serving

God this way until one comes to the level of end purpose of that thing, which is the level of Shabbat, the world of souls.

People who have great minds can do this.

But smaller people like us are on a very low level, referred to as the level of feet, and we cannot attain such knowledge.

Therefore we must yearn to have a leader of the generation, a faithful shepherd, who will have the strength to illumine within us the knowledge of how to come to the purpose. This leader must be like Moses, who, because of his high level, was able to illumine even the lowest of the low, even a maidservant. As our sages said, "A maidservant saw at the Red Sea what Ezekiel the prophet didn't see" (*Mechilta Beshalach* and Rashi there; and see *Zohar Beshalach* 44 and *Vayikra* 22).

Even Ezekiel, who was a great prophet, did not see what a maidservant saw in the days of Moses.

This was all due to the great level of the leader, Moses. The leader can illumine even the feet, which are so far from the brain. The people on the level of feet can then know the purpose through the acts of God in this physical world.

Through the greatness of the leader, one can draw the mind down to the feet. Those feet may then be higher than another mind.

This is referred to in the verse, "Come and see" (Psalms 46:9). "Come" – i.e., feet that can come and walk; they shall see the "acts of God Who destroyed the [enemies'] land." "The acts of God that He placed in this land" – i.e., in this low world. Via the acts of God in this low world, one can know the purpose.

This is referred to in the words "Who has destroyed the [enemies'] land." Our sages tell us that the word *destroyed* – *shamot* – can also be read as *sheimot* – "names" (*Berachot* 7b). And "names" is related to the idea of the purpose of the world. How? The word *purpose* – *tachlit* – is the acronym of the phrase, "the purpose of the creation of heaven and earth." [We also see that a "name" is related to the soul of a thing,] as in the verse, "The soul of a living thing is its name" (Genesis 2:19).

In other words, the world of souls, which is the purpose, is clothed in this low world.

One attains the goal precisely through this low world.

The attainment of the ultimate, the attainment of God, is dependent on the creation of the low world. All souls must pass through this world in order to attain the ultimate. "The Messiah, son of David, will only come when all souls have passed through a body" (*Yevamot* 62b). All of us must come to this low world in order to attain the ultimate.

Everything in the world is necessary, so that through it one may reach the ultimate.[7]

---

7. Source: *Likkutei Moharan* 2:39.

37

Messiah

The Test of the End of Days

Rabbi Nachman said that great heresy will spread throughout the world.

Fortunate is the person who will strengthen himself with faith in those times.

He said that his warning of heresy and his exhortation that one must strengthen oneself with faith will not help. There were others, such as Daniel, who foretold that before the coming of the messiah, many will be tested and refined, that the evil will worsen, while the wise will have understanding, and so on.

Rabbi Nachman foretold that this would be a test before the coming of the messiah. Many would be tested and refined in their faith. The person who would pass the test and retain his faith would be fortunate and would attain all the good that is destined to come to us (may it be soon and in our days), about which the prophets and wise men prophesied.

If so, everyone should take care to remain strong in his faith. Since this prediction is already common knowledge, there will be no test.

But nevertheless, this will still be a great test.

Many will do evil. As the verse says, "The wicked will act wickedly" (Daniel 12:10).

"I am telling this in advance for the sake of those few good people who will be strong in their faith. They will have great internal battles. But my words will console and strengthen them, for they will see that someone already predicted this."[1]

⋘

Greatness in the End of Days

Rabbi Nachman said that there will be a time that a simple, kosher person will be as extraordinary as the Baal Shem Tov was in his day.[2]

⋘

Calculating the Coming of the Messiah

A number of Torah leaders have calculated the time of the messiah's coming. In our time, people said that various events meant that the messiah would soon come; and this has also occurred in previous generations.

Rabbi Nachman didn't agree with this. He said that every time people say the end has come, it is certain that the messiah will not come.

The *Zohar* has already cursed all those who calculate the end, for the son of David will only come when people are distracted (*Sanhedrin* 97a). Now people are saying that the messiah will come in 5600 (1839–1840), and they imagine that there are hints to that effect in the holy *Zohar*. But he is certain not to come at that time. Perhaps he will come before 5600, or

---

1. Source: *Sichot Haran*, no. 35
2. Source: *Sichot Haran*, no. 36.

afterward, but not in 5600, because everyone is looking toward that date.

Whenever people say that the messiah will come at a certain time, he won't come then.

But he will come and he will not be delayed, speedily and in our days, when people are completely distracted, when no one will be calculating that time as his coming. Then he will suddenly arrive.[3]

€€€

The Messiah Will Come Suddenly

Rabbi Nachman said that the messiah will come suddenly. There will be a great cry that the messiah has come. Everyone will throw aside his business. The banker will cast aside his business, and the candlemaker will cast aside his wax. As the verse says, "They will cast aside their gods of silver and gold" (Isaiah 2:20).[4]

€€€

Nature Will Not Change

It isn't true that, as some people think, the world will be different than it is now after the messiah comes. He [will be here,] and everyone will be ashamed of his foolish actions.[5]

€€€

Even the Messiah Will Die

People think that there will be no more death after the messiah comes. This is not so. Even the messiah will die.[6]

---

3. Source: *Chayei Moharan* 2:61, no. 81.
4. Source: *Chayei Moharan* 2:74, no. 145.
5. Source: *Chayei Moharan* 2:74, no. 175.
6. Source: *Chayei Moharan* 2:13, no. 35.

❮❮❮

My Fire Will Burn until the Messiah

Even though Rabbi Nachman said, "My fire will burn until the messiah will come," every Bratslaver must arouse himself every day. There are various explanations of the word "burn," "*t'luen*." Even if only a few small sparks are left from the fire, that too is considered "burning."[7]

❮❮❮

We Have Already Tasted the Good Wine

Once a great merchant traveled with fine Hungarian wine. His servant and wagon driver told him, "We are traveling with this wine, and we are suffering so much. Give us some wine to taste."

He gave them some of the wine.

A while later, this servant happened to be among wine drinkers in a small town. The others drank some wine and praised it highly, saying that it was Hungarian wine.

The servant said, "Let me try some."

When they gave him some, he said, "This isn't good Hungarian wine at all."

They were angry and rebuked him. But he answered, "I know that this isn't good Hungarian wine because I have already had much better." But they didn't pay any attention to him.

Rabbi Nachman said, "In the future, when the messiah will come, when this old wine is given to others, they will be fooled; one will be able to give them Wolochian or Stravitzer wine, and tell them that it is good wine. But our people cannot be fooled, for we have already tasted the good wine."[8]

---

7. Source: *Avanehah Barzel*, p. 70.
8. Source: *Chayei Moharan* 2:10, no. 20.

≪≪≪

The Messiah Will Be One of My Offspring

Rabbi Nachman said, "What will happen with me, I do not know. But I have accomplished this with God: the righteous redeemer will be one of my offspring."

He said this in public.

He admonished us to honor his children, for they are precious trees, from whom will grow good and wondrous fruits.

He said that he took his offspring from the high spiritual level of *Atzilut* (Emanation).[9]

≪≪≪

The Days Preceding the Messiah

On the evening following Shabbat *Teshuvah*, 5570 (1809), people were talking about the messiah. People were saying that he would come that year.

But Rabbi Nachman did not agree. He said then that before the messiah comes, people will generally not be crying out about faith. "Although there will be a number of *tzaddikim* then who will be crying out in a great voice about faith as I am today, until they become hoarse, it will not help."

The verse says, "Whoever remains in Zion and the remnant in Jerusalem will be called holy" (Isaiah 4:3). Our sages commented, "In the future, *tzaddikim* will be called 'holy' in the same way that God is called holy" (*Bava Batra* 75b)—in the simple sense of the word.

Without a doubt, the *tzaddikim* then remaining who will be strong and maintain their holy faith will be fit to have even more said about them, because they will keep their faith and will not allow themselves to fall and be led astray.

There will be a number of false leaders. It is clear that there

---

9. Source: *Chayei Moharan* 2:13, no. 34.

will not be a group of people, like us today, who really want to hear the word of God. There will be a number of kosher people in the generation, but they will be scattered.

"Write this as a remembrance in a scroll" (Exodus 17:18), so that people will be aware in the days to come that someone knew this ahead of time. This will help them strengthen their faith in God and in His true *tzaddikim*.[10]

---

10. Source: *Sichot Haran*, no. 126.

38

The Land of Israel

Struggling to Come to the Land of Israel

Rabbi Nachman said that a person who desires to be a Jew – that is, to go from level to level – can only do so via the land of Israel. When one is victorious, one is called a warrior. Before one is victorious, "let the one who is girding himself not praise himself like the one who is taking off his belt" (1 Kings 20:11). Only after one is victorious is one a warrior.

After Rabbi Nachman finished this teaching, I asked him, "What were you referring to when you mentioned that the land of Israel is so great and going there constitutes the concept of victory?"

He grew curt with me and answered, "I meant the land of Israel in its simple meaning – with its houses and buildings." His whole intent in describing the level of the land of Israel was the actual land of Israel to which Jews travel. It was his desire that every Jew – whoever really wants to be a Jew – should travel to the land of Israel. Even if one had many obstacles, one should break through them all and go there; for when one manages to come to the land of Israel, one achieves the essence of victory.

Rabbi Nachman encouraged me a great deal and inspired me to break through all my many obstacles. As a result, I myself traveled to the land of Israel. . . .

"He who is putting on his belt should not boast like the person who is taking it off" means that a person has to undergo many sufferings and obstacles before he arrives at the land of Israel.

Once, when Rabbi Nachman was speaking of the many obstacles and dangers that he had undergone in Istanbul, he told us that we can come to the land of Israel easily.

We would not have obstacles such as he did. If we wanted to, we could go to the land of Israel easily. But we too must be prepared to suffer and to break through obstacles before arriving, for, as our rabbis taught, the land of Israel is one of the three things that were given with suffering.[1]

Once, Rabbi Nachman said that there are people who imagine that they are really yearning to come to the land of Israel – if they could travel in comfort. But this is not a perfect desire. A person who truly desires to come to the land of Israel needs to go even by foot. As Abraham was told, "Go" – meaning "walk."[2]

€€€

My Place Is in the Land of Israel

Rabbi Nachman said, "My place is only in the land of Israel. In all my travels, I am only traveling to the land of Israel, and for the moment, I am a leader in Bratslav and other places."[3]

€€€

The Quality of the Land

Rabbi Nachman said that when he had been in the land of Israel, some outstanding men had told him that before they had moved

---

1. The other two are Torah and the world-to-come.
2. Source: *Chayei Moharan* 1:12, no. 15.
3. Source: *Chayei Moharan* 1:68, no. 6.

there from eastern Europe, they couldn't imagine that the land of Israel was in this world. They had thought that its holiness as described in our holy Torah made it an entirely different world. (For instance, the Torah delineates all the borders of the land of Israel because of its great and awesome holiness.) They weren't able to imagine that the land of Israel was in this world until they arrived and saw it.

The land of Israel is exactly like other countries, and its soil has exactly the same appearance as the soil of other countries. Sometimes, people bring white soil from the land of Israel. But that soil is only found in particular spots – and one can find white soil in Europe as well.

In appearance there is no difference whatsoever between the land of Israel and other countries. But it is nevertheless exceedingly holy, at the apex of holiness. Fortunate is the person who has walked four cubits there, as our sages have said.[4]

⋘

He Suffered More from His Love

When Rabbi Nachman was in Haifa, a young Moslem came to him and spoke to him a great deal. Rabbi Nachman didn't understand what he was saying. This Arab stayed with Rabbi Nachman for every meal, day and night, and treated him warmly.

Once, he came to Rabbi Nachman in great anger, carrying a weapon, and began to shout at him. But Rabbi Nachman didn't understand what he was saying.

A woman from Volichia was there. As soon as the Moslem left, she told Rabbi Nachman that for God's sake he should flee from that house, for the Moslem had challenged Rabbi Nachman to a duel.

Rabbi Nachman fled to the house of a well-known *chasid*, Rabbi Ze'ev of Charni Ostroho, who hid him in an inner room.

The Arab again came to Rabbi Nachman's inn. He said,

---

4. Source: *Likkutei Moharan* 2:116.

"Where is that man? Tell him that I like him very much. I will give him donkeys and my horse so that he can go with the caravan to Tiberias. He doesn't have to be afraid of me any more."

So it was. Rabbi Nachman came to his inn, and the Arab came and didn't say anything to him. He only smiled and laughed, and he treated Rabbi Nachman very warmly and with a great deal of friendship.

This episode of the Arab was quite extraordinary.

Rabbi Nachman said that he suffered more from the Arab's love than from his hatred and anger.

According to what we heard from his holy mouth, he was in great danger from this Arab. He apparently said that this Arab was the devil himself, but that with God's mercy he was saved from him.[5]

❮❮❮

The Tune of the Land of Israel

Rabbi Nosson heard that Rabbi Nachman was once informed about the journey of the holy rabbi of Berditchev to Iassi, and how he had amassed a great deal of money.

Rabbi Nachman said, "A tune is better than this. And a tune of the land of Israel is certainly better than this.

"If one took a person with a lust for money and showed him a tune of the land of Israel, this lust would be nullified before it."[6]

---

5. Source: *Shivchei Haran*, Rabbi Nachman's Journey to the Land of Israel, p. 17.

6. Source: *Chayei Moharan* 2:70, no. 133.

39

Holy Days

The Great Wedding

Rabbi Nachman said that Shabbat is like a great wedding. Everyone is rejoicing and dancing with great joy.

One person is standing to the side, dressed in clothing that doesn't keep out the cold. He runs up quickly and wants to come in and rejoice.

But one needs great merit even to see [the wedding] through a little crack.[1]

❥❥❥

The Holidays and Rabbi Nachman's Chair

Before Rosh Hashanah of 5569 (1808), the slaughterer from Teplik brought Rabbi Nachman a beautiful chair. At that time, Rabbi Nachman told of a vision or dream in which he had been brought a chair surrounded by fire, and everyone in the world—

---

1. Source: *Sichot Haran*, no. 254.

men, women, and children—came to see it. When they left, connections formed between them, and marriages were arranged. Also, all the leaders of the generation went to see it.

Rabbi Nachman said, "I asked, how far is it? And why were marriages arranged so quickly?"

I circled around them to go there, and I heard that Rosh Hashanah was coming.

I didn't know whether to return or to remain where I was. I said to myself, "How can I remain here on Rosh Hashanah? But because my body is so weak, why should I return?" So I remained.

I came to the chair and saw Rosh Hashanah itself, as well as Yom Kippur itself and Sukkot itself.

I also heard cries, " 'My soul hates your new month and holiday celebrations' (Isaiah 1:14). Why should you judge the world? Rosh Hashanah itself will judge."

Then everyone, together with all the leaders of the generation, fled.

I saw that all the images of all the creatures in the world were carved on the chair. Each one was carved together with its mate next to it. That is why marriage arrangements had been made so quickly. Every one found and saw his mate there.

Since I had previously been learning, it occurred to me that the verse, "His throne is flames of fire" (Daniel 7:9) was the acronym of *shadchan*, matchmaker. Via the chair, matches were made. Also, the word for throne is an acronym for Rosh Hashanah, Yom Kippur, Sukkot.

That is why Shmini Atzeret is the marriage of the Matron.

I asked, "How will I make a living?"

I was told that I would be a matchmaker.

The fire surrounded the chair.

In truth, Rosh Hashanah is very good. It is the holiday during which the moon hides—which is why God says, so to speak, "Bring an atonement offering for My sake." This is very good for the world, for then, we ourselves ask for atonement on Rosh Hashanah.[2]

---

2. Source: *Chayei Moharan* 1:39, no. 4.

≪≪≪

The *Dreidel*

The entire world is like a spinning *dreidel*.

Everything turns around and changes: from man to angel and angel to man; from head to foot and foot to head; everything is revolving and changing from one thing to the next, from top to bottom and from bottom to top.

In truth, everything is in its root one.

There are *nivdalim*, separate beings – that is, angels, which are totally separated from physicality. And there are *galgalim*, heavenly beings; these are physical, but very fine. And there is *shafel*, the low world – that is, our world, which is complete physicality.

Even though each one of these three things is taken from its own place, everything is in its root one.

Therefore, the entire world is a revolving wheel, and everything goes around and changes. Now something is at the top like a head and something else is at the bottom like a foot. Afterward, the foot becomes a head and the head becomes a foot; man becomes an angel and angel becomes a man. As we find in the Talmud, angels were cast down from the heavens to this world, and they became completely physical, lustful creatures. Other times, angels came to this world and invested themselves in physicality. On the other hand, we find that people were transformed into angels.

This world is a turning wheel (see *Shabbat* 151b), which is a *dreidel*, and everything turns around.

In truth, everything is in its root one.

(Besides this, the foot of one thing may be higher than the head of another. The same refers to the spiritual universes. The lowest level of the highest world is higher than the highest level of a world lower than it. But everything is a turning wheel.)

This is why people play with a *dreidel* on Hannukah. Hannukah is related to the idea of the Temple [for the Jews fought to regain the Temple and when they did so, they lit the *menorah*, which burned miraculously for eight days].

The essence of the Temple is this idea of the revolving wheel.

The Temple is the level of the upper level coming down below and the lower level rising above (see *Bava Batra* 10b). God rested His presence on the Tabernacle, and afterward on the Temple. This is the level of the upper level coming down. The entire form of the tabernacle [and the Temple after it] was based on a supernal form. This is the idea of the lower level rising up.

This is the idea of a *dreidel*, a turning wheel, where everything is transformed.

Via philosophy, it is very hard to understand how God, Who is so exalted and higher than all spirituality, could constrict His presence from the highest heavens into the space of the tabernacle. Nevertheless, God showed that He is the opposite of what philosophers imagine, and He placed His presence in the tabernacle.

Also, it is very difficult to understand through philosophy that a human being, who is so low, should have the power to make an impression in the upper worlds, or that a low animal should be offered as a sacrifice that will please God. This is God's will – but how can God have a will?

In truth, however, God demonstrated the opposite of what the philosophers believe. He placed His presence below in the tabernacle and the Temple, and the animal sacrifices were pleasing to Him.

This is the level of the upper level coming down below and the lower level rising above; the level of a turning wheel; the level of a *dreidel*.

Philosophical works mention a hyle. This is a state between the potential and the actual. Everything is at first *in potentia*, and afterward it becomes actualized. When it leaves potentiality but is not yet actualized, it is at the level of the hyle. This hyle thus is the root of all created beings. All created beings that come from there are in one of three categories: separate beings (*nivdal*), heavenly beings (*galgal*), and lower beings (*shafel*) – all of them revolving and changing from one to the other, for everything is in its root one.

This idea is expressed by the letters on the *dreidel*: *hey, nun, gimel, shin*. These letters are the acronym of the following four words: hyle, *nivdal* (separate being), *galgal* (heavenly being), and *shafel* (low being). These four words describe the four aspects of creation, all of which revolve and are transformed constantly.

This is hinted at on Hannukah, because Hannukah commemorates the dedication (*hannukah*) of the Temple, where above was below and below was above, which is the *dreidel*, the revolving wheel, things changing from one state to another.

These transformations are the level of the redemption.

Therefore, when the Jews were redeemed from Egypt, they sang at the song of the sea, "You will bring them and plant them on the mountain of Your inheritance" (Exodus 15:17), referring to the Temple. The essence of redemption is that there will be a Temple building, where exists the level of the revolving wheel, of the upper level coming down below and the lower level rising above.

This is the idea of the ultimate.

In truth, all is one. In its source, all is one.[3]

€€€

The Holidays Call Out

God's will is revealed through the holidays. Every holiday declares [God's] will—i.e., the fact that everything happens only as a result of His will. This is referred to in the phrase, "A holy calling" (Leviticus 23:7)—the holiday itself calls and declares [God's] will.

On every holiday, God performed great miracles, which are the opposite of nature. Through this, His will is revealed—i.e., the fact that everything is due to His will and that nature does not make anything necessary.

On Passover, God took us out of Egypt with great signs. On Shavuot, He gave us the Torah with great signs. On Sukkot, we were surrounded by the clouds of glory.

Thus, every holiday declares and calls out God's will, on the level of "*a holy calling.*"[4]

---

3. Source: *Sichot Haran*, no. 40.
4. Source: *Likkutei Moharan* 2:4:6.

40

Secular Learning

The Voice of the Holiday and the
Forehead of the Snake

The call of the holiday, which reveals God's will, is not always heard. Only to the extent that one feels and hears the voice of the holiday, which declares God's will, does one experience a corresponding level of joy.

When God's will shall be revealed—that is, the fact that everything depends on His will—then people will realize that God will judge the Gentiles' imposition of the exile and redeem us from their hand.

But when one believes that everything is necessitated by nature, then justice isn't a factor, since everything follows the rules of nature.

This is referred to in the verse, "The righteous man will rejoice, for he has seen vengeance; he will wash his steps in the blood of the wicked" (Psalms 58:11). "His steps"—*pa'amav*—refers to "the three times—*p'amim*—in the year" (Deuteronomy 16:16), which are the holidays, through which God's will is revealed. Through this, "the righteous man will rejoice, for he has seen vengeance." As the verse says, "Then man will say, there is payment for the righteous, there is a just God in the world" (Psalms 58:12). It has been revealed that there is a God Who judges with His will; there is a reward for the righteous; and He will take vengeance.

As a result, "the righteous man will rejoice."

This is the level of the joy of the holiday, via the revelation of God's will, which is revealed when the voice of the holiday declares God's will.

But not everyone hears the voice of the holiday. There are evil beasts that trample and claw. These are the scientists who demonstrate with their mistaken intellect that everything is ruled by nature, as though there is no will of God.

They say that even the great miracles that God performed for us are ruled by the laws of nature.

These scientists are like evil animals that trample and claw many of our people, who are drawn to believe that everything is necessitated by natural law.

When these scientists grow stronger, their roar rises and overwhelms the voice of the holiday that declares God's will. Then the joy of the holiday is silenced, since the joy of the holiday results from the revelation of God's will.

This is referred to in the verse, "Your troublers have roared in the midst of Your Temple – mo'ed; they have made their signs into signs [i.e., they have placed their banners in the place of the holy symbols of the Jews]" (Deuteronomy 74:4). The roar of the troublers, that is, the voice of the evil animals, the scientists, entered into the holidays – mo'adim – that is, into the call of the holiday that declares God's will.

The troublers roar that everything is ruled by natural law. Natural law is symbolized by the signs of heaven. This is referred to in the words, "they have made their signs into signs." They have made the signs of the heavens into signs, saying that everything runs only in accordance with the signs of heaven, or natural law.

These evil beasts, the scientists, are subjugated by the great wise man in holiness, who can connect all wills to the root of will, which is the level reached at the time of Moses' death (*Zohar Yitro* 88b, see *Zohar Naso* 129a). This is the level of the forehead of will [which can also be translated as "favor"], the level of "It will be on his forehead constantly to gain favor" (Exodus 28:38). One must connect all the wills in the world to the source of will.

In this way, one conquers, subjugates, and crushes the opinions of the scientists . . . who deny God's will.

In opposition to this, the source of science is called the "forehead of the snake." Everything has a source, and the source of science is the forehead of the snake. This is on the level of "a brass plate—*mitzchat nechoshet*—upon [Goliath's] feet" (1 Samuel 17:6). *Mitzchat nechoshet* can be read as meaning, "forehead of the snake." Goliath was a heretic who wanted to show that everything is caused by nature alone, which is the forehead of the snake.

"[Goliath's] feet" is the level of "cause." In the verse, "God blessed you because of me" (Genesis 30:30), "because of me" literally means "to my foot." In that verse, Jacob told Laban that God brought about the blessing through him and because of him. So we see that "foot" is the level of "cause."

Jacob attributed all causes to God. But Goliath attributed all causes to the forehead of the snake, to the laws of nature. This is referred to in the words, "and a brass plate upon his feet."[1]

❦❦❦

The Unhappy End of Scientists

Rabbi Nachman said that whoever reveals a new wisdom—that is, a secular, worldly wisdom—comes to a bad end and has a downfall through that wisdom, as we found among many of the scientists who made new discoveries. For instance, Columbus, who discovered the land of America, in the end died in chains as a result, for he was denounced to the king, as is told in the history books. The scientist who invented a technique for

---

1. Source: *Likkutei Moharan* 2:4:6–7.

avoiding thunder died of thunder. The one who created an extraordinary viewer was ultimately burned in consequence. Socrates, the head of the early philosophers, was poisoned because of his wisdom. Many philosophers who made new discoveries as a result suffered a downfall.[2]

⋘

We Do Not Need to Make New Things

I heard Rabbi Nachman say that he doesn't agree with those great Torah learners who want to derive new laws or customs, and whose intent, rather than being toward the real truth, is to come up with novellae. He said that the desire to create new things is a lust typical of great people. He didn't agree with this at all. We do not need to make new things. A person's intent should be for the real truth.[3]

⋘

A Proof of the World's Creation

Once, Rabbi Nachman told us that there is a proof that the world was created [and hasn't existed eternally]. If not, where would there be room to hold all the creatures in the world? We see clearly that the human population keeps expanding. From one person come thousands and tens of thousands of generations. This is true of every individual. If so, the whole world should have been entirely full, and there would be no place in the world, which is limited and finite, to hold people, since they keep increasing to such an extent.

Another time, he gave another proof, this one from the dead. When a person dies and is buried in the ground, he adds to some degree to the ground. Even after his body decays, a little is added

---

2. Source: *Chayei Moharan* 1:78, no. 10.
3. Source: *Chayei Moharan* 1:78, no. 10.

to the ground. If the world was infinitely old, it should have grown so large that it would have reached the sky and gone yet higher, according to the foolish and wrong opinion of the heretics. If so, how would there be room in the world to hold what endlessly keeps getting added, according to their foolish opinion? There would be no room to hold them.[4]

⋘

Guarding One's Mind

A person must guard his mind from non-Torah influences. In addition, he must continuously renew his mind.

When one renews one's mind, one renews one's soul, for the mind and the soul are one.[5]

⋘

Avoiding All Secular Influences

One must completely remove oneself from books that follow the path of the Greek sciences – i.e., their secular investigations and wisdoms – no matter who wrote them.[6]

⋘

The Inferiority of Science and Philosophy

Rabbi Nachman very much disparaged the books of scientists and philosophers. He said that they do not contain the perfect intelligence that one finds in works of the *Maharsha*, the *Maharam Shif*, and other holy books that contain great depth and wisdom. Secular books do not contain such wisdom. They are built only on logical structure by means of which they arrive

---

4. Source: *Chayei Moharan* 2:40, no. 11.
5. Source: *Likkutei Moharan* 1:35:2.
6. Source: *Likkutei Eitzot*, Talmud Torah, no. 46.

at some proof. But they do not possess the wisdom of our holy Torah.

Rabbi Nachman said, "Fortunate is the person who doesn't know anything about those books, but who walks in simplicity and has fear of punishment. The first stage in serving God is fear of punishment. Without this fear, it is impossible to begin serving God. Even *tzaddikim* need this fear. Very few people serve God out of love. The higher level of fear, which is awe of God's greatness as ruler, cannot be attained by everyone. Most people must serve God through fear of punishment.[7]

"When a person learns the books of the scientists and philosophers," said Rabbi Nachman, "doubts and heresy enter his heart. Every person is born with evil, for the [lower] nature of a person is drawn from [corporeality—]that is, the evil desires of this world. Only through fear of punishment does he break these desires and begin to go on the way of God.

"But when he learns those books, he finds statements of doubt and heresy that aid his own natural evil.

"We have never found that any person has ever been made a kosher, God-fearing person by reading books of science, even though those books speak of great things. Such books are vanity, for they confuse a person a great deal and do more harm than good."

Rabbi Nachman said that Moses chose a very good portion for us. When he gave us the Torah, he began it with "In the beginning, God created the heavens," without any scientific proofs. He just commanded us to believe in God with simple faith. It is completely forbidden to study the scientific method.

Even though the holy *Zohar* disparages fear of sin, our ethical literature teaches that this is an essential method in serving God.

Rabbi Nachman said that the techniques and inventions that the philosophers and scientists created, such as weapons and so on, came from above. It would not have been possible for them to invent anything if they had not received a spark of wisdom from above. When the time came for a particular insight or

---

7. This may be different in our era, as Rabbi Kook points out (see Introduction).

invention to be revealed, it was sent into their minds from above.

Earlier scientists had investigated the same matters. Why didn't they discover these techniques and inventions? The answer is that everything comes from above. When the time comes for something to be revealed, then its wisdom shines on the scientist who makes the invention.

But scientists do not receive this light from a holy place; rather, it comes to them via the demonic side. This is self-understood.

Also – not to mention the two in the same breath – one can only interpret the Talmud when the interpretation is sent from heaven. Everything is from above. Everyone receives insights from a higher place.

There are tens of thousands of levels from which a person receives illumination and sparks.[8]

---

8. Source: *Sichot Haran*, no. 5.

Maimonides points out that through studying nature, one can gain a deep appreciation of God's greatness. Furthermore, the Vilna Gaon claims that to the extent that one lacks secular learning, one's understanding of Torah will be impaired a hundredfold. Secular studies should be a vehicle for coming close to Torah and God.

And more than that, any secular learning undertaken with the intent of serving God itself becomes imbued with holiness and may therefore no longer be considered secular, as Rabbi Norman Lamm says in *Torah Umadda* (Northvale, NJ: Jason Aronson, 1990).

However, Rabbi Nachman seems to posit a dichotomy between two paths: the path of good, which is that of Torah; and the path of evil, which is that of secular learning.

According to some, such as the late Rabbi Shlomo Freifeld of Yeshiva Sh'or Yashuv in Far Rockaway, Rabbi Nachman's statements were culturally limited and can be understood only in the context of his society.

Rabbi Nachman lived in the late eighteenth and early nineteenth centuries, when science was being used as a tool in a *Kulturkampf* against traditional values and beliefs. For a Jew to learn science was to make a major break with his upbringing, ambience, and culture. It was an act of rebellion. This was especially true of Rabbi Nachman's specific milieu in the Ukraine, where the Jews were particularly unsophisticated and pious. If Rabbi Nachman had lived in one of the more sophisticated communities of Poland, Rabbi Freifeld speculated, his attitudes and pronouncements could well have been different. In a massively imbalanced society, Rabbi Nachman had to be imbalanced to the other extreme, merely to keep things even.

Today, however, our upbringing and consciousness are radically different. Science is not a foreign value being thrust upon us. Rather, we have grown up with popular science and many of its assumptions— both those in consonance with and those antithetical to Torah beliefs. Science, including its analytical, experimental model of viewing and testing things in this world, is a part of us. This may give us a strength that the Jews of Rabbi Nachman's milieu may not have had. Being extremely pious and not trained to think critically, any attempt at critical thinking put them at risk of also applying their skepticism to the Torah, to whatever small extent. But we have a secular background and training that can allow us to retain critical thinking while believing in God. This is an ideal that goes back to Maimonides and the Vilna Gaon: the ability to serve God with simple faith but not at the expense of the intellect.

Furthermore, science itself has been evolving radically. Rabbi Nachman was relating to a science that had left the moorings of belief in God and had undertaken an actively anti-Providence position. Everything was to be attributed to natural law and "God was a postulate that was not needed."

But today, over the past eighty or so years, science has been slowly shifting so that rather than being a rival to Torah values, it is beginning to acknowledge positions acceptable to Torah belief. Ideas dealing with the reality of nonmaterialism, such as Rupert Sheldrake's speculation on the morphogenetic field, are attracting attention. Some scientists argue for the presence of apparent purpose and predestiny, or predisposition, in the universe. In *Genesis and the Big Bang* (New York, Bantam, 1990), George Schroeder, a leading physicist, reconciles cosmological theories with Genesis. Again, it is beginning to be possible to appreciate God through the wonders of nature.

Some say that Rabbi Nachman's statements on science were often passing remarks made in a casual setting. Other remarks were presented in a form meant to be understood by simple people.

One can say that Rabbi Nachman held the position, predicated on his position of radical spirituality, that since by definition science declares laws of nature, it is troubling to the apprehension of Godly life force in all things, which is their real nature. Whether or not Rabbi Nachman's own understandings of physical reality are true is irrelevant to this basic point. Rabbi Nachman is a poet, not a scientist. In our own day, when so much of our surroundings are cut off from nature, and we live science fictional lives in our cities closed off from nature, ruled by fax machines and personal computers, locked into commuter trains and environments of fluorescent lighting and air conditioning, and surrounded by sophisticated, electronically produced music, we are entering a life not only enslaved to the belief that God's nature rules over God's will, but that man's reality has replaced God's nature. In this cacophony of artificiality, Rabbi Nachman's radical spirituality is a refreshing voice.

Rabbi Nachman's statement that scientific insights come from the side of nonholiness is reasonable in his worldview that anything that does not promote, and that tends to denigrate, a consciousness of God is negative. Influences can either come from a positive, holy source or a negative, unholy source. Therefore, science must come from a negative, unholy source. Why can't there be an intermediary force of neutral energy? Perhaps the answer is that this would be nature; but the idea of nature, which divides a person's consciousness from God, is itself ultimately negative.

It is typical of Rabbi Nachman's idealistic outlook radically opposing the idea of this-worldly reality that he defines all science as stemming from a negative source. Science declares the rule of natural law. Even if a scientist declares himself a believer in God and says that God is working through these rules, he has brought the level of reality and consciousness down to a point where it is assumed that God has to work through nature. Rabbi Nachman consistently spoke from the viewpoint beyond nature. Any position that would tend to make a person rely on immutable laws of nature, rather than seeing nature as a malleable tool of God, has its roots in the "forehead of the snake." The snake is the entity that enticed mankind with the belief that by partaking of something in this world, they too could attain a godly status.

Even within classical Torah Judaism, Rabbi Nachman's approach is a radically isolationist one. In his all-encompassing yearning for total spirituality, Rabbi Nachman denied the reasonableness and efficacy of all other wisdoms.

Rabbi Nachman states that no one has ever come to serve God through books of science, and that the bad in those books outweighs

the good. As for the first statement, Maimonides notes, as quoted
earlier, that one of the primary ways a person can come close to God
is through understanding the greatness of nature. Rabbi Nachman
states that it is better to eschew such literature altogether and simply
learn Torah. Whereas this technique can work for an extremely small
coterie, it is certainly not true for the vast majority of reasonable
human beings. Only a small, intense group of disciples can deny all
scientific insights and believe simply, uncritically, and literally all the
statements of this kind in Torah sources.

Indeed, many people have left Torah Judaism, or been repulsed by
it, precisely because of narrow attitudes decrying scientific knowledge
that seems to contradict Torah statements, with an appeal to *ad
hominem* attacks, emotion, and simple faith, often violating a person's
sense of reason and denying his own good intent in wondering about
those contradictions. When doubt is based on reasonable questions and
faith is based on denial of one's own perception of reality, one comes to
either deny one's own thoughts and adopt a repressive attitude toward
others, or else break away from that system of faith.

For some personalities, societies, or eras, secular learning may be an
occupation that is detrimental to one's spiritual life. However, for
others, it seems that the opposite is true. For them, secular knowledge
is an essential component of their ability to serve God in a full and
healthy manner.

Rabbi Nachman opens many doors for a Jew to serve God. Intellec-
tually, it gives him many new tools to make connections to God in his
learning. Emotionally, it gives him many tools to connect to God with
hope and joy. It encourages and strengthens a person.

But does Rabbi Nachman also insist that a person close doors within
himself? Does he tell a person, Close the door of your intellect, and
your trust in your own perception?

If one believes that Rabbi Nachman's approach of rejecting science
and accepting his ideas of how the material world works as accurate
cannot be changed and is relevant in its simple sense in all generations,
then the answer is yes. But if one believes that Rabbi Nachman presents
a paradigm that is malleable, considering one's circumstances, then
one can learn from him and maintain one's own intellectual freedom
and will.

Rabbi Nachman opposed not only secular and scientific studies, but
any philosophical inquiry, including the teachings of great Jewish

philosophers, such as Maimonides. According to one opinion, Rabbi Nachman wanted to exclude those teachings that came through human intellect as opposed to divine inspiration – whether science or philosophy. He wished Jews to apprehend the level of Torah (based on Kabbalah) that comes not from human intellect but from direct acquisition of heavenly knowledge and insight.

41

Rabbi Nachman's Teachings

Traveling Words

Rabbi Nachman said, "Sometimes, when I say something to someone, my words don't have an effect. They travel from one person to the next until they finally come to a particular person and enter his heart very deeply. Then they have their full effect and awaken him."[1]

❊❊❊

Barrels of Medicine

Rabbi Nachman told a parable to explain why he told so many wondrous and awesome teachings, stories, and talks, even though it doesn't seem that they are having as much of an effect as they should.

There once was a king whose only son grew so ill that all the doctors despaired of healing him.

---

1. Source: *Sichot Haran*, no. 208.

One day, a very great physician came, and the king begged him to try to save his son.

The physician answered, "To be completely honest, it is very unlikely that your son can be saved. But still, there is one thing that you can try. But I don't know whether to tell you about it, because it won't be easy."

The king begged the physician to tell him what to do.

The physician said, "Your son is so desperately ill that it is impossible to put even a drop of medicine into his mouth.

"Now there are some drugs that are so expensive that just a small vial costs tens of thousands. You will need to fill barrels full of these precious drugs, and then pour full buckets over your son. You understand that all of these expensive drugs will be wasted. But still, your son's body will be strengthened a little bit. And perhaps while the drugs are pouring over him, a drop will trickle into his mouth. This may possibly heal him."

The king immediately agreed to do this and commanded that the physician's instructions be carried out.

As a result, the king's son was healed.

The moral is self-understood. Precisely because we are so spiritually ill, the *tzaddik* (the physician) must pour precious medicine over us, even though it seems that almost all of it goes to waste. Still, a good odor remains. And perhaps, over the course of many days, we will be able to swallow one precious, wondrous drop, and we will have the hope to be completely cured, both spiritually and physically.[2]

€€€

Chambers within the Palace

Before Shavuot, when I came to Rabbi Nachman from Nemirov together with my friend, Rabbi Naftali, Rabbi Nachman spoke to me. It appeared to me that he was upset that I was coming to him too often. At that time I was traveling to him very frequently.

As soon as I entered and found him in his large house that was

---

2. Source: *Chayei Moharan* 2:32, no. 51.

next to the *beit medrash*, he said to me, "Hello and goodbye," and he smiled slightly.

Afterward, he remained sitting in his place, which was next to the door that was right outside the old *beit medrash*. He spoke with me and comforted me very much. He told me, "How do you know what God wants to make of you? Today you are this way, and afterward, you will be. . . ."

He said, "You will become. . . ." He hinted that I would be in great danger many times without number, almost to the point of. . . . "But," he said, "I will open the paths of intelligence, and you will go and travel through all my teachings, like a person goes through palaces and wondrous buildings."

Then he explained the matter to me a bit.

He told me that his teachings are constructed so that it is as though the person learning them enters a palace that contains chambers, rooms, porticoes, and gateways that are wondrously beautiful, with many floors of different types and different architecture. As soon as one enters one room and begins to look around and admire the beautiful, new things there, one sees that another wondrous door has been opened to another room. And so one goes from room to room, from room to upper story, and so on. Doors and windows connect them all in a wondrous order, with deep wisdom and with the greatest charm and beauty.

(All this can only be understood only by a person who has begun to understand somewhat the depth of Rabbi Nachman's words.)

"Still," Rabbi Nachman said, "it will not be yours. Rather, it will be as though you are walking through someone else's property. But I want it to be yours entirely – and it will be. You may think that this will be due to your good deeds. This isn't so. It will only be so because I want it that way."[3]

---

3. Source: *Chayei Moharan* 2:72, no. 142.

42

A Complete Teaching from *Likkutei Moharan*

Learning Torah, Seeing Godliness in Everything

"Fortunate are those who are wholesome in their way and who walk in the Torah of God" (Psalms 119:1).

Via the Torah, [God accepts] all entreaties. [Also,] the grace and importance of Israel are elevated before all people, whether one is dealing with them in spiritual or in temporal matters.

At this time, because of our many sins, the true grace and importance of Israel have fallen and are lodged with [the Gentiles]. However, via the Torah, the grace and importance of Israel may be elevated.

Torah is called "a lovely sheep and a graceful mountain goat" (Proverbs 5:19). Torah [is called "graceful" because, as our sages say,] "it gives grace to those who learn it" (*Eiruvin* 54b). One [gains grace by learning Torah,] and then all of one's entreaties are accepted.

A Jew must always look into the intelligence that resides within every object, with the intention of connecting himself to that wisdom and intelligence. That intelligence will shine for him. Then, he will be able to come close to God through the object.

This intelligence is a great light that can illumine a person in all his ways. As the verse states, "The wisdom of a person illumines his face" (Ecclesiastes 8:1).

This is connected to Jacob. Jacob attained the birthright, which is called the "beginning," and the word "beginning" is equivalent to wisdom, as in the verse, "The beginning of wisdom" (Psalms 111:14) (*Tikkunim* 14; *Zohar Mishpatim* 121b). Also, the Bible states, "[Jacob] tricked me twice" (Genesis 27:36). The word "tricked" comprises the root of Jacob's name. And Onkelos's Aramaic translation of "tricked" is "acted wisely."[1]

[Intelligence] is also connected to the concept of the sun. A person's intelligence illuminates him in all his ways, just as the sun does. As the verse says, "The way of the righteous is like a clear light, growing brighter with the coming day" (Proverbs 4:18).

In addition, [intelligence] is connected to the Hebrew letter *chet*, which comprises the Hebrew word for life, *chiyut* (see *Zohar Pinchas* 245a:, and *Tikkun* 65). Wisdom and intelligence are the living force within every object. As the verse says, "Wisdom gives life" (Ecclesiastes 7:12).[2]

However, [one cannot easily see the intelligence within every object.] This is because the light of intelligence is [overwhelmingly] great. As a result, one can only gain access to it via the [spiritual force indicated by the] Hebrew letter, *nun*. *Nun* refers to [God's] royal power. (As the verse says, "Under the sun, [the king's] name will rule" (Psalms 72:17). [The word for "rule" is "*yanun*," which is related to *nun*.] Rashi translates *yanun* as "royalty.")

This royal power is related to the moon. The moon has no light of its own. Its only light is that which it receives from the

---

1. So again there is a link between Jacob and intelligence.
2. So this intelligence is analogous to light, Jacob, the sun and life.

sun (*Zohar Vayichi* 238a, 249b). [In this way, the moon is analogous to the spiritual level referred to as] royalty, which also "has nothing of its own." All it has is what it receives from the living force, which is related to the letter *chet* and analogous to wisdom and the sun.

[When the connection between the *chet* and the *nun* is made,] "the light of the moon becomes equal to the light of the sun" (Isaiah 30:26). [This is a messianic, redemptive goal.][3]

However, if a person doesn't connect himself to the intelligence, wisdom, and living force in every object, he is on the level of Esau. This is because, as the verse says, "Esau despised his birthright" (Genesis 25:34), the "birthright" being intelligence.

[Esau's rejection of this intelligence] is referred to in the verse, "The fool does not desire understanding, but only the uncovering of his heart" (Proverbs 18:2). Such a level is the "royalty of evil," [which is the negative counterpart of the positive royalty connected to Jacob]. It is also a level of the "moon of evil," [the negative counterpart to the positive moon mentioned above]. The verse says about this "moon of evil," "The moon was shamed [. . . for the Lord of Hosts ruled]" (Isaiah 24:23) (see *Tikkunim* 8).

[These opposing forces of Jacob and Esau, the royalty of good and the royalty of evil, and the moon of good and the moon of evil,] are analogues to a person's good inclination and his evil inclination.

The good inclination is [homiletically] referred to as "a poor and wise [child]" (Ecclesiastes 4:13) (see Rashi and see *Zohar Vayeishev* 179, and *Midrash Rabbah Kohelet* and *Nedarim* 32b). [This child] is the level of royalty, which is "poor, with nothing of its own," except for what it receives from wisdom.

On the other hand, the evil inclination is called "an old and foolish king" (Ecclesiastes 4:13). This is the royalty of the side of evil, which does not desire intelligence and wisdom. As quoted above, "The fool does not desire understanding."

---

3. So one must connect oneself to the intelligence in every object via the medium of the letter *nun*, which is analogous to royalty and the moon.

Every individual has to give power to the royalty of holiness in order to vanquish the royalty of evil. As our sages said, "A person should always arouse his good inclination to overcome his evil inclination" (*Berachot* 5a).

And how can one give power to this holy royalty? Via learning Torah vigorously. (As our sages said, "A person should always arouse his good inclination. . . . If [the evil inclination] leaves, fine. If not, the person should learn Torah.") Also, our sages said that "if the corrupt [evil inclination] meets you, drag it to a study hall" (*Kiddushin* 30b).

By learning Torah, a person gives strength to the royalty of holiness. Then this royalty, which corresponds to the letter *nun*, receives the life force, which corresponds to the letter *chet*, from wisdom. These two letters join together and, [since these letters symbolize the moon and sun,] "the light of the moon becomes equal to the light of the sun."[4]

"And when [the power of holiness] rises, [the power of evil] falls" (Rashi on Genesis 25:23). Therefore, the royalty of evil falls and is liquidated. As the verse states, "For the ways of God are straight; the righteous will walk in them and sinners will stumble in them" (Hosea 14:10). The "ways of God" refers to Torah. Through Torah, righteous people cling to the royalty of holiness. They are strengthened. But "sinners will stumble in them." "Sinners" refers to the royalty of evil and the evil inclination. As a result of the [study of] Torah, this [evil] experiences a downfall.

Then, all of one's entreaties[, whether of God or of man,] are accepted.

The main reason a person's entreaties are not accepted is that they have no grace. As a result, they do not enter the heart of the one whom one is entreating. It is as though there is no room in that person's heart for these words to enter.

But via the Torah, the letters *chet* and *nun*, [symbolizing wisdom and royalty,] are joined. Then they spell out the word *chen*, which means "grace." That is why the Torah is called "a

---

4. Then the power of holiness is elevated.

graceful mountain goat." Then a person's words are infused with grace, and his prayers and entreaties are accepted.

This is like someone who speaks graceful words that enter the heart of the person whom he is entreating.

When the *chet* and *nun* join together, they form the word *chen* (grace). This brings about the level symbolized by the letter *tav*. *Tav* refers to carving and making an impression. (We see this in the verse, "And you shall make a sign" (Ezekiel 9:4). The word for "sign" is "*tav*.")

Via [words of] grace, one carves a place in the heart of the one who is being entreated. Then there is room for one's words to enter and to be accepted. This carving and making an impression are called *tav*.

All this is referred to in the verse, "The words of wise men are heard in calm" (Ecclesiastes 9:17). The word for "calm" is *nachat*, which is made up of the three letters, *nun*, *chet* and *tav*—i.e., the word *chen* plus the *tav*. Together, they form the word for "calm," meaning that one's words are listened to and one's prayer is accepted.

As mentioned above, Jacob is the level of intelligence. As a result, Jacob achieved the level of grace. As the verse says, "God has been gracious to me" (Genesis 33:11). Similarly, when Jacob blessed his sons, the fathers of the twelve tribes of Israel, he blessed them with grace: "These are the children with whom God graced your servant" (Genesis 33:5).

At the time Jacob made this last statement, Benjamin was not yet born. Therefore, Benjamin was later blessed with grace by Joseph, who told him, "May God give you grace, my son" (Genesis 43:29) (see *Breishit Rabbah Vayishlach*, chap. 78; *Mikeitz*, chap. 92). It was precisely Joseph who could bless Benjamin with grace. This is because Joseph in particular[, among all of Jacob's sons,] incorporates within himself the various characteristics of Jacob. As the verse says, "These are the generations of Jacob: Joseph" (Genesis 37:2) [, implying that] Joseph is the essence of Jacob's offspring.

In fact, Jacob and Joseph are considered to be one (see *Zohar Vayailach* 176b, *Vayeishev* 182b). Joseph is described as "his

firstborn ox, beauty is his" (Deuteronomy 33:17). "Firstborn"
refers to intelligence, as mentioned previously. "Ox" in Hebrew,
"*shor*," is related to the word "*shor*" that means "gazing." In
other words, one must "look" into the "intelligence" that is in
every object. "Beauty is his"–Onkelos's Aramaic translation
reads, "he is illumined." In other words, one's intelligence
illumines one in all matters.

One's intelligence illumines one even in a place that is entirely
dark. This occurs when one looks at the intelligence that lies
within every object. Then that intelligence brings one close to
God.[5]

"Rabbi Bar Bar Chana said: 'There is a wave that sinks a ship.
This wave has a crest of white fire.' (*Rashbam* explains: This
white fire is a destructive spiritual force.) [The wave] is beaten
with a rod on which is carved [God's name,] I Am That I Am
(Exodus 3:14)."

The "wave" refers to the evil inclination (cf. *Kehillat Yaakov*).
This wave "sinks a ship."

The ship is "grace and importance." The word for ship,
"*s'fintah*," is related to the word *safun*, which refers to something hidden and important (*Mo'ed Katan* 28).

The evil inclination wants to sink the grace and importance of
Israel, which is their holy royalty.

"This wave has a crest of white fire." At first, the evil
inclination disguises itself in good deeds. It fools a person into
thinking that it is urging him to do good. This is referred to by the
"crest of white fire," [since the color white symbolizes holiness].
Nevertheless, [as *Rashbam* points out,] it is really "a destructive
spiritual force."

"[The wave] is beaten with a rod on which is carved [God's
name,] I Am That I Am." The most basic way to overcome the
evil inclination is through [learning] Torah. The Torah is[, in a
mystic understanding,] entirely composed of names of God
(*Zohar Emor* 89b). The entire Torah is related to the letter *vav*
(see *Zohar Pekudei* 226b). We see that the tablets of the law[,

---

5. Now that the basic structure of this teaching has been presented,
it is applied to the interpretation of a rabbinical allegory.

which are an emblem of the Torah,] were six handbreadths by six handbreadths in size (*Bava Batra* 14). [The number six is in Hebrew indicated by the letter *vav*. So we see that the Torah is related to *vav*.] This letter *vav* refers to the "rod upon which was carved I Am," which symbolizes the names of God, which comprise the Torah.

The letter *vav*, [being a straight line,] is in the shape of a rod. And it is composed entirely of names of God. In other words, the holy Torah subjugates the evil inclination, whose intent is literally to drive a person insane. This is because a sinner is considered to be insane. As our sages say, "A person will not commit a sin unless a spirit of foolishness has entered him" (*Sotah* 3a).

People who are literally insane are beaten with rods and given amulets with names of God. The Torah that a person learns is like those rods and amulets. With them, one subjugates the evil inclination and drives out the insanity and spirit of foolishness that had entered him. [In other words, a person's basic drive is to be good and to serve God. Any contrary drive is not part of his basic personality, but an added, imposed level. Through learning Torah, a person relates directly to and reveals his core personality, which seeks to be close to God. As a result, the imposed drives that distracted a person from God flee.] This is referred to in the allegory as "[The wave] is beaten with a rod on which is carved [God's name,] I Am That I Am" (see *Midrash Rabbah Kedoshim*, beginning of chap. 25).[6]

"Happy are they who are wholehearted in the path."

"Happy" is in Hebrew *ashrei*. This word can be related to *shor*, meaning, "to gaze."

---

6. Rabbi Nachman is not endorsing this particular method of dealing with insane people. He is bringing an example from everyday life to illustrate a spiritual process. From a mystical perspective, there is nothing in this world that does not have its analogue in the spiritual spheres. Because this method of treating insane people existed, Rabbi Nachman found it meaningful as an analogy to the battle with one's evil inclination.

Now Rabbi Nachman applies the basic structure of this teaching to the verse from the Book of Psalms that was quoted at the very beginning.

"Those who are wholehearted in the path." This is related to
Jacob, of whom the verse says, "And Jacob was a wholehearted
man" (Genesis 25:27). Jacob is intelligence.

In other words, one should gaze upon the intelligence that is in
every object. This intelligence is related to Jacob, who "was a
wholehearted man."

One can do this by learning Torah. That is why the verse in
Psalms continues, "who go in the Torah of God."

By learning Torah forcefully, one empowers the royalty of
holiness, which is the letter *nun*, to receive from intelligence,
which is the letter *chet*.

Then "grace" (*chen*) is formed, and one's entreaties are accepted.

Then, the grace and importance of Israel is elevated. And all
their prayers and entreaties are accepted.[7]

---

7. Source: *Likkutei Moharan* 1:1.

Appendix

Azamer Bish'vochin
אזמר בשבחין

13. AZAMER BISH'VOCHIN — אזמר בשבחין

K'rivu shoish'vinin, 'aviydu tikunin, l'afosho zinin, v'nunin im rachashin:

L'm'ebad nish'mosin, v'ruchin chad'tin, b'sartein uvis'losin, uvis'loso shiv'shin:

V'iturin shav'in loh, umalkah dil'eilo d'yis'ateir koilo, b'kadish kadishin:

R'shimin us'simin, b'goi kol 'almin, b'ram Atik Yoimin, halo batish batishin:

Y'hei ra'avo kamei, d'yishrei 'al 'Amei, d'yis'aneig lish'mei, bim'sikin v'duv'shin:

Asadeir l'droimo m'narto dis'simo v'shulchon im nahamo, bits'foina ar'shin:

B'cham'ro goi chaso um'donei aso l'orus va'arusa, l'hitakfo chaloshin:

l'hitakfo chaloshin .....

N'ateir loin kisrin, b'milin yakirin, b'shav'in iturin, d'al gabei cham'shin:

Sh'chin'to tis'ator, b'shis nahamei lis'tor, b'vovin tis'kator v'zinin dich'nishin:

Sh'visin ush'vikin, m'so'avin dir'chikin, cha'vilin dim'ikin, v'chol zinei char'shin:

Bibliography

Augros, Robert M., and Stanciu, George N. *The New Story of Science*. New York: Bantam Books, 1984.

Avraham ben Nachman of Tulchin and Horowitz, Shmuel. *Kochavei Ohr, Avanehah Barzel*. Jerusalem: Hasidei Breslov, 5732.

Hacohen, Tzaddok. *Tzidkat Hatzaddik (Hamalei)*. Jerusalem: Yad Eliyahu Ki Tov, 5747.

Kaplan, Aryeh. *Until the Mashiach — The Life of Rabbi Nachman: An Annotated Chronology*. Ed. Dovid Shapiro. Jerusalem: The Breslov Research Institute, 1985.

Nachman of Bratslav and Nosson of Nemirov. *Hishtapchut Hanefesh*. Ed. Nosson of Nemirov. Jerusalem: Meshech Hanachal, 5744.

Nachman of Bratzlav. *Likkutei Eitzot*. Ed. Nosson of Nemirov. Jerusalem: Keren Hadpasa Dihasidei Breslov, 5736.

Nachman of Bratzlav. *Likkutei Moharan*. Jerusalem: Meshech Hanachal, 5750.

Nachman of Bratzlav. *Likutey Moharan*. Vol. 1. Trans. Rabbi Simcha Bergman. Jerusalem: Breslov Research Institute, 1986.

Nachman of Bratzlav. *Likutey Moharan*. Vol. 1b. Trans. and ed. Moshe Mykoff. Annot. Chaim Kramer. Jerusalem: Breslov Research Institute, 1989.

Nachman of Bratzlav. *Outpouring of the Soul: Rabbi Nachman's Path in Meditation*. Ed. Nosson of Nemirov. Trans. from *Hishtapchut Hanefesh* by Rabbi Aryeh Kaplan. Jerusalem: Breslov Research Institute, 1980.

Nachman of Bratzlav. *Rabbi Nachman's Stories*. Trans. of *Sippurei Maasiyot* with notes based on Breslover works, by Rabbi Aryeh Kaplan. Jerusalem: Breslov Research Institute, 1983.

Nachman of Bratzlav. *Sefer Hamidot*. Jerusalem: Zvi Latzaddik, 5745.

Nachman of Bratzlav. *Sippurei Maasiyot*. Brooklyn: Hasidei Breslov, 5736.

Nachman of Bratzlav. *The Gems of Rabbi Nachman*. Trans. and ed. Rabbi Aryeh Kaplan. Jerusalem: Yeshivat Chasidei Breslov, 1980.

Nachman of Bratzlav. *Vehilchata Kinachmani*. Ed. Yaakov Dov Halevi. New York: Zeicher Naftali, 5738.

Neier, Moshe Tzvi. *Chayei Harayeh*. Tel Aviv: Moriah, 5743.

Nosson of Nemirov. *Chayei Moharan*. Brooklyn: Hasidei Breslov, 5734.

Nosson of Nemirov. *Rabbi Nachman's Wisdom*. Trans. of *Sichot Haran*, by Rabbi Aryeh Kaplan. Ed. Rabbi Zvi Aryeh Rosenfeld. Jerusalem: Breslov Research Institute, 1973.

Nosson of Nemirov. *Shivchei Haran, Sichot Haran*. Benei Brak, 5736.

Nosson of Nemirov. *Tzaddik: A Portrait of Rabbi Nachman*. Trans. of *Chayei Moharan* by Avraham Greenbaum. Ed. Moshe Mykoff. Jerusalem: Breslov Research Institute, 1987.

Schneerson, Menachem Mendel. Rosh Hashanah talk of 5728 [1968]. Reprinted for Rosh Hashanah 5752 [1991]. Brooklyn: Otsar Hahasidim, 1991.

Schneerson, Yosef Yitzchak. *Likkutei Dibburim*. Brooklyn: Otsar Hasefarim, 1980.

Solomon, Benzion. *Azamer Bishvachin: Rebbe Nachman's Songs*. Vol. I:1: *The Traditional Music of Chasidei Breslov, Shabbos Evening: Part I*. Jerusalem: Breslov Research Institute, 1988.

Index

About the Author

Y. David Shulman has written a number of biographies for young adults, most recently *The Maharal of Prague*. His translation of Rabbi Ovadiah of Bartenura's travel letters has been published as *Pathway to Jerusalem*. His poetry has appeared in such publications as *Modern Haiku* and *Response*, and he is the editor of the occasional journal *TAL — Torah Art and Literature*.